KICKING
In the
WALL

KICKING In the WALL

A YEAR OF WRITING EXERCISES, PROMPTS, AND QUOTES TO HELP YOU BREAK THROUGH YOUR BLOCKS AND REACH YOUR WRITING GOALS

BARBARA ABERCROMBIE

New World Library
Novato, California

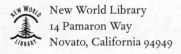 New World Library
14 Pamaron Way
Novato, California 94949

Text design by Tona Pearce Myers

Library of Congress Cataloging-in-Publication Data
Abercrombie, Barbara.
 Kicking in the wall : a year of writing exercises, prompts, and quotes to help you break through your blocks and reach your writing goals / Barbara Abercrombie.
    pages   cm
Includes bibliographical references.
ISBN 978-1-60868-156-3 (pbk. : alk. paper) — ISBN 978-1-60868-157-0 (ebook)
 1. Fiction—Authorship. 2. Creative writing. I. Title.
PN3355.A25 2013
808.3—dc23   2013004763

First printing, May 2013
ISBN 978-1-60868-156-3
Printed in Canada on 100% postconsumer-waste recycled paper

 New World Library is proud to be a Gold Certified Environmentally Responsible Publisher. Publisher certification awarded by Green Press Initiative. www.greenpressinitiative.org

10 9 8 7 6 5 4 3 2 1

For my students

I would go as far as I could and hit a wall, my own imagined limitations. And then I met a fellow who gave me his secret, and it was pretty simple. When you hit a wall, just kick it in.

— PATTI SMITH

CONTENTS

INTRODUCTION

This is a book of exercises — warm-ups and side doors into stories, ways to kick down the walls and surprise yourself with where your writing can go. The best way to approach the exercises is to give yourself a five-minute time limit for each writing prompt. If you get on a roll, you can always keep writing, of course. And if you don't, so what? You've only spent five minutes on it. You can tear it up; it's just an exercise.

In my writing classes and workshops, we do a lot of five-minute exercises. The only rule is that you have to keep your pen moving for the whole five minutes, no stopping to correct what you've written or to think about what to write. When you do this, you get out of your own way; you let the process of writing take over. Amazing things can happen; I've seen novels, memoirs, and many essays get started with the five-minute exercises. And a lot ended up being published.

Oddly, directions and boundaries (seemingly the antithesis of creativity) can help you get into your stories.

No writer has the time to wait around for inspiration, but inspiration has a way of arriving when you're already writing.

A year's worth of exercises follows, 365 one-line prompts and longer exercises to get you going. There are quotes to inspire you, and in the second part of the book are examples of what my students came up with for some of the exercises. (You may want to wait until after you try the exercises yourself to read them.)

If you're writing fiction, give the "you" in the prompts to one of your characters, and see what he or she has to say. New glimpses of your characters, unexpected details, sudden ideas, can expand your fiction. Let your characters surprise you when you use them for the exercises; see where your story can go when you loosen up.

Whenever you veer off into another topic in an exercise, just follow your own instincts and keep going. Do them alone, or with a writing buddy, or in a group. Do one a day, five once a week, or ten over a weekend. Write them in your journal or in a special notebook, or start a new file on your computer. Whatever works best for you. You're not taking a test; you're just exercising.

KICKING
In the
WALL

Writer's block is not a problem for me, ever. It comes from being diverted…by outside considerations, such as self-censoring, fear, and accepting the dictates of others.… The cure is to do exercises.

— KATE BRAVERMAN

1. Jot down the details of your wall or whatever stands between you and the page. Close your eyes and envision it. Maybe it's a real wall you see — gray, thick, and impenetrable. Or maybe it's a voice you hear — a teacher or parent, or possibly your own voice. Imagine a concrete image or sound, then note whatever details or pictures float into your head. Is the wall thick? Flimsy? Covered with ice? If you hear negative voices, what are the words? If you have a kitchen timer, you might set it for five minutes, or just check your watch or a clock. Take a deep breath and don't think — go for five minutes.

2. Write an intention, a new way to look at the block or wall that's keeping you from writing, or a plan to ignore it and move on. Maybe you have a description of a formidable wall, or a negative monologue, or maybe just random words scattered on the page. It doesn't matter, as long as you write something, anything, for five minutes. Could your wall also be giving you privacy and protection? Or maybe you need to blast a hole in it or dynamite it to smithereens. It's your wall; you get to decide how to handle it.

> *The hardest part is the first three sentences. Sitting down with pen and paper and just getting those first three sentences out; I sometimes have to write my way into something knowing that the first paragraph is just preliminary, but I have to write myself in. It's like being in a cold lake and sometimes you have to go in toe by toe. Some of you can plunge in, but not always; you have to write your way into it. And then you're swimming.*
>
> — MADELEINE L'ENGLE

3.   Write three sentences. They don't have to connect. They don't even have to make sense. Just three sentences.

4.   Write about a time you went into cold water — a lake, pool, shower, or rain. Write about how your body reacted. Was it delicious relief from the heat, or a shock that caused goose bumps and made your lips turn blue? Or write about the cold water as a metaphor.

I'm trying to cause people to be interested in the particulars of their lives because I think that there's one thing literature can do for us. It can say to us: pay attention. Pay closer attention.

— RICHARD FORD

5. Write what your five senses are picking up right at this moment. Keep it simple. You don't have to write down thoughts or feelings — just the specific details of sound, touch, smell, taste, and what you see. Years from now those simple, specific details will bring back this moment to you.

6. Write about a time you tried to pay attention but couldn't. You floated out of your head, or you fell asleep, or you studied your fingernails. What was it you didn't want to pay attention to? What was it you were avoiding? Or was boredom part of it?

> *What I wanted was some dreamlike Frank Lloyd Wright bungalow where we could sit on the veranda forever and it would always be twilight in the temperate zones, in the most beautiful house.*
>
> — WILLIAM KITTREDGE

7. Where do you live? In a house, in a town, in a dream? Be literal or not. The photographer Dorothea Lange once gave her students an assignment to photograph where they lived. They asked her to do the assignment too; she brought in a picture of her foot. (She'd had polio as a child.) Go with your first thought.

8. What is the landscape of your heart? What place moves your soul? Flat desert and dry heat? Mountains and pine trees? City streets? The Midwest or the New England you grew up in? Or maybe a landscape that you've only read about or seen in a film. Don't think; trust whatever comes up for you.

9. Write about a place you lived in as a child. If you can't remember the details of a house or apartment, make them up. Often when you start writing about the past, things you think you can't remember will come back to you.

> *Moving unleashes fear, yes, but it also provides as compensation the potential for boldness, bravery, and newfound strength.*
>
> — LOUISE DeSALVO

10. Write about a time you moved from one house or town to another. Either with fear and anxiety, or with boldness, or a combination of both. Write about packing and unpacking, the smell of cardboard boxes, fresh paint, or mildew in the new place. Write about what got broken or what was lost.

This is the one thing that stays the same: my husband got hurt. Everything else changes. A grandson needs me and then he doesn't. My children are close then one drifts away. I smoke and don't smoke.

— ABIGAIL THOMAS

11. What is the one thing in your life that stays the same? Is it a huge event like an accident or illness that changed your life forever? Or is it something ordinary, so familiar that it's like wallpaper.

12. What changes constantly in your life? What leaves you breathless sometimes? What is it that you want to hold on to?

> *There are two relationships I have with the outside world — one is with my hair, and the other is with the rest of me.*
>
> — VERONICA CHAMBERS

13. Start with the words "My hair..." Is there anyone on earth who is totally happy with their hair? If you are, write about it. If you aren't, write about it. If you're writing fiction, what do you know about your character's hair?

> *I find that if I don't give shape to my experience in language, if I don't spend time in the crafting and honing of that experience in words, I don't feel real to myself.*
>
> — MARK DOTY

14. Write about a time you weren't sure who you were. Maybe when you were a kid and pretending to be someone else. Or maybe as an adult when you were in the wrong relationship or job.

15. Write about your favorite Halloween costume. Did you go trick-or-treating in the costume? Did you feel transformed — more powerful or more beautiful? Or did you feel hidden and safe?

> *It's a curious risk, fiction. Some writers choose fantasy as an approach to truth, a way of burrowing under newsprint and formal portraits to find the despair that can stow away in a happy childhood, or the affluent grace of a grandfather in his undershirt. In the final accounting, a hundred different truths are likely to reside at any given address.*
>
> — BARBARA KINGSOLVER

16. Write about a moment of despair you felt as a child. Try giving the moment to a child with a name different from yours. Write in the third person. It can be fantasy or the truth — or somewhere in between. And if you can't remember a childhood moment of despair, write about not remembering.

17. Write about a lie you told as a child.

18. Write about a childhood birthday — the presents, the cake, the games, the guests. Or write about birthdays never celebrated.

19. Write about a time you were unfairly accused of doing something wrong.

20. Write about a time you did something wrong and got away with it.

We need stories to live, all of us. We live by story. Yours enlarges the circle.

— RICHARD RHODES

21. Start with the words "I remember the time Mom/ Dad/my brother/my sister…" Nothing is too trivial or silly or serious to remember. See how many stories you can come up with. Maybe you've never even thought of these experiences as stories; it was all just stuff that happened. Writing down the details and remembering those times can lead to shaping the stuff that happened into a story.

> *Before I wrote the book, I wondered: Am I going to get in trouble? Will I be perceived as a dirty woman?...And you know what? Nothing bad happened, everyone liked it, it was fine. The secret is: You don't need to keep it secret.*
>
> — CAITLIN MORAN

22. Write about a time you got into trouble. How deep was the trouble? What was the worst thing that happened?

23. Write about a time you worried about something, but then nothing happened. Did you feel foolish? Relieved? Disappointed?

> *The world begins at a kitchen table. No matter what, we must eat to live.*
>
> — JOY HARJO

24. Write about your mother's kitchen. Was the kitchen the heart of your home or the scene of conflict? Did your mother's kitchen shine, or were there dirty dishes in the sink? Did it smell like things baking or things burning? Or maybe there was no mother.

25. Write about your father's kitchen. Did he just open the fridge occasionally for a beer, or was he the cook and caregiver? Or wasn't there a father?

26. Write about your current kitchen table or counter. Is it piled with newspapers, a catchall for your stuff? What has been the most important discussion at that table? What are the best and the worst memory of what's taken place in your kitchen?

Help one person at a time, and always start with the person nearest you.

— MOTHER TERESA

27. Write about a time you tried to help someone by giving advice. Write the dialogue, the urgency of the advice, the reaction of the person you were advising. Write about what was at stake.

28. Write about a time you tried to mend fences. Write about what had been broken. What stood in the way of the mending?

Your absence has gone through me
Like thread through a needle
Everything I do is stitched with its color.

— W. S. MERWIN

29. Who or what do you miss? Does it feel like a needle? Or like an empty space in your heart?

30. Write about a time someone didn't show up. Did you feel disappointment or worry or relief?

31. Write about a time when you realized something you did became a habit. Did it feel like a chain? Or was it a good habit, something you had worked hard for? When and how did it go from cobweb to cable, from fragile to unbreakable?

32. Write about a ritual in your life. Does your ritual come from needing to feel safe, or is it done to celebrate something, to remember, to care for someone or something, to follow a religion — or for another reason?

When I wrote something wrong I always took it to mean that something was wrong with me, and when something was wrong with me I lost my nerve, my focus, and my will.

— J. R. MOEHRINGER

33. Write about a time when you felt something was wrong with you — either physically or in your head. Maybe you were sick, or maybe you felt crazy.

34. When something was wrong, what did you lose? Your nerve? A sense of safety? Did you plow on, or did you give up? ·

The key is to be here, fully connected with the moment, paying attention to the details of ordinary life. By taking care of ordinary things — our pots and pans, our clothing, our teeth — we rejoice in them. When we scrub a vegetable or brush our hair, we are expressing appreciation: friendship toward ourselves and toward the living quality that is found in everything.

— PEMA CHÖDRÖN

35. Write about an ordinary action — housecleaning, gardening, taking a bath, washing a car, doing dishes, cooking — as a mindful act. If you're writing fiction, this exercise can be a way to learn more about your characters — how do they clean house (or not clean house)? Do any of them have a garden? Indoor plants? Do they cook, and if so, what do they love to cook most? Do they take baths or showers? The details we create for our characters inform our fiction, whether on the page or not.

36. Pay attention to an ordinary action you do today, and then write about it. Focus on verbs, not adjectives.

> *My shoes are worn out, and the friend I live with at the moment also has worn-out shoes. When we are together we often talk about shoes. If I talk about the time when I shall be an old, famous writer, she immediately asks me "What shoes will you wear?"*
>
> — NATALIA GINZBURG

37. Write about a pair of worn-out shoes you own. Write about the miles you've walked in them, where and when you bought them, why you still have them.

38. Write a memory of a pair of shoes you had in grade school. Or write about not remembering anything about shoes you wore as a child.

39. Write an opening of a scene with someone asking a question about a pair of shoes.

40. Write about how you will live when you're an old, famous writer.

The most regretful people on earth are those who felt the call to creative work, who felt their own creative power restive and uprising, and gave to it neither power nor time.

— MARY OLIVER

41. Write about a time you felt called to do something creative but ignored it. Were you too busy to heed the call? Or were you afraid? Or were you too busy because you were afraid?

42. Write a list of small regrets. Or write about one huge regret.

Actually, the real secret was stranger than wanting to write a book. The real secret was that I already thought of myself as a writer. I'd hardly written a word and I couldn't think of a single idea for a book, but in my mind, I was a writer. I'd been a writer since I was seven.

— SUSAN RICHARDS

43. Write about when you decided you were a writer. Or when you realized you wanted to write.

44. Write about the real secret.

45. Write about a time you felt self-pity. How did you handle it? Wallow on the page as much as you want. You have permission to wallow until you come to the end of it. Maybe you'll even find some humor in it as you write.

> *If life is made easy by technology, it is made meaning-*
> *ful by observance of its rites of passage: the baptisms*
> *and marriages and funerals — those rich and deliber-*
> *ate idioms by which we are pronounced alive, in love,*
> *gone but not forgotten.*
>
> — THOMAS LYNCH

46. Write about a rite of passage, religious or not, that you observed or took part in — a birth, a relationship recognized by a community, or a death. Write about the details of the ritual, the emotion, the surroundings, the weather.

47. Write about a nontraditional wedding. Yours or one you attended or one that you've dreamed about.

All well-brought-up people are afraid of having any experience which seems to them uncharacteristic of themselves as they imagine themselves to be. Yet this is the only kind of experience that is really alive and can lead them anywhere worth going. New, strange, uncharacteristic, uncharted experience, coming at the needed moment, is sometimes as necessary in a person's life as a plough in a field.

— KATHARINE BUTLER HATHAWAY

48. Write three adjectives that describe you.

49. Write about a strange experience you had that was totally uncharacteristic of how you imagine yourself to be. How did it make you feel? Ashamed? Free? Uncomfortable? Exhilarated? Or maybe you'll discover how you really felt as you write about it.

I had a strange thought this morning. If I were to imagine myself walking through the upper floor of a large house with different parts of myself in different rooms, which door would I be afraid to open, what self would I be afraid to meet?

— PHYLLIS THEROUX

50. Write about the part of yourself that you're avoiding or are afraid to meet. Imagine a series of closed doors, and in the different rooms behind the doors are the different parts of yourself. Maybe the different parts are you at different ages, or the various roles you play in your life, or what you consider to be the real you versus the public you.

51. Write about opening one of the doors and being surprised at the self you discover.

Arrival. The rust. The launch: white and gray, banged about, roughly painted, old paint. A general rundown air. The waiting crowd massed in the terminal; the colours of the ladies' clothes.

— V. S. NAIPAUL

52. Write about a time you arrived in a new place. Paint the scene with unfinished sentences.

> *My work is strung on moments when I realize something*
> *— a novel is, by nature, one long Realization, which is*
> *not to say other pursuits aren't dependent on discovery:*
> *sailing is. Cooking is. Playing music is. Sex always is.*
> *Loving is a series of discoveries: it starts, significantly,*
> *with a Realization....If writing were as exciting as*
> *falling in love, I'd get a lot more written.*
>
> — MARIANNE WIGGINS

53. Write about a time you realized something significant about sex. Something you might have discovered while making love. Or a discovery you made when you didn't or couldn't make love.

54. Write a scene in which your character cooks breakfast and makes a discovery.

55. Write about a time you fell in love. Maybe with the love of your life, or maybe it was an intense, short-lived infatuation.

The journals are a way of finding out where I really am.... They are not dependent on the muse.... They sort of make me feel that the fabric of my life has a meaning. What often seems fairly meaningless, like weeding a patch in the garden, when I write it into the journal, it sort of becomes something else.

— MAY SARTON

56. Write about the fabric of your life. Be literal or think of it as a metaphor. Is your life fraying, stretched, or tucked in tightly? Cotton, wool, silk, polyester, cashmere? Are buttons missing, or is it covered with sequins? Ironed or wrinkled?

57. Write about a time your life unraveled.

58. Write a list in your journal of ten ordinary things you did yesterday. If you don't already keep a journal, start one today.

> *I understood that living itself had a deadline — like the book I had been working on. How sheepish I would feel if I couldn't finish it. I had promised it to myself and to my friends. Though I wouldn't say this out loud, I had promised it to the world. All writers privately think this way.*
>
> — ANATOLE BROYARD

59. Write to a friend, promising him or her the book you're going to write or are writing. Don't send the letter, but as you write, consider why this particular person would be interested in your book.

60. Write about a deadline you missed once. How did you feel in the days leading up to the missed deadline — panicked or resigned? Were there consequences?

61. Write yourself a deadline for the story you're writing or are about to write. Be specific. Include the schedule for your writing and how you'll meet this deadline.

Their story, yours, mine — it's what we all carry with us on this trip we take, and we owe it to each other to respect our stories and learn from them.

— WILLIAM CARLOS WILLIAMS

62. Write the story of your life in five minutes. That's not a typo. Five *minutes*.

63. Write the story of your life in four thousand words, taking all the time you need. This length should make you stretch beyond the comfortable and familiar story you tell strangers about your life.

The way we tell our life story is the way we begin to live our life.

— MAUREEN MURDOCK

64. Write a scene from your life, putting a slightly different spin on things. Maybe making yourself a little tougher or more sensitive. Braver or more honest, or with a better sense of humor.

Day 7: Roast Chicken, Corn Bread Dressing, White Beans, Spinach Salad, Fruit Salad, Carrots, Rolls, Coconut Cake

— GWEN ROLAND

65.   Write about the best meal you had this week. Write about the worst meal. Food immediately gives us something specific to write about. Try this exercise in your journal when there seems to be nothing to write about.

66.   Write what a fictional character loves to eat for breakfast, lunch, and dinner. Find food that you don't usually eat, and write why the character loves this food.

67.   Write about your favorite and least favorite lunch when you were a child.

68. Write the questions of a cat, a dog, or a chicken. What are the questions? What are the answers? Make them as bizarre as you can. Loosen up. Have fun. Pretend you're back in kindergarten.

> *What you need to know in writing and what you need to know in art...you have to know where the funny is, and if you know where the funny is, you know everything.*
>
> — SHEILA HETI

69. Write a fictional scene or a scene from real life, and find the funny in it. If you can't exaggerate, or make it lighter, or find irony or dark humor in the scene, write about why this scene can't possibly be funny.

Our stories help us understand a terrifyingly confusing and dangerous world, most of which is a riddle. For the world to feel safe, we need to make sense of it, especially when we encounter setbacks and misfortunes that shatter our confidence....How we tell our story influences how we feel about ourselves. Change your story and you change your identity.

— Diane Ackerman

70. Write about a time your confidence was shattered.

71. Write about resurrecting your confidence. Write about a time you were brave. A time you showed kindness. A time you tried to do the right thing.

72. Write an emotional experience from your life, and change your reaction to it. Maybe it was when you let yourself be a victim and caved in. Or maybe you were unkind and a bully when being sensitive was called for.

Here the world was black, and so you were just you; you could discover all those things that were unique to your life without living a lie or committing betrayal.

— BARACK OBAMA

73. Write about a place where you felt you could just be you. Start with the words "Here the world was..." Write about why these people understood you, what you were part of, why you felt at ease.

74. Write about one thing that you feel is unique to your life.

It needs a very moon-like consciousness indeed to hold a large family together regardless of all the differences, and to talk and act in such a way that the harmonious relationship of the parts to the whole is not only not disturbed but is actually enhanced.

— C.G. JUNG

75. Write about a large family gathering at a holiday dinner where someone is attempting to create a harmonious relationship but the opposite is occurring. Write about the food. Write some dialogue — real or imagined. Write about old grudges and slights.

> *Yearly, for the past ten years, a friend of mine has told the tale of how she lost her virginity. At first the details were scant and prosaic. A guy named John. An apartment in New York. But my friend discovered embellishment and, endowed with a gift for swift improvisation, she inflated her story out of proportion, an immense balloon improbably bobbing in an annual parade.*
>
> — BERNARD COOPER

76. Write about losing your virginity. Use scant details, mainly unembellished facts.

77. Write about losing your virginity, with dramatic and embellished details. Dramatize and inflate the event, real or imaginary.

78. Write about a time you didn't lose your virginity. Write about the disappointment, or the restraint and discipline shown. Write about why you didn't lose it.

> *Somehow I had to believe that doing some work, in a wrong way, was better than doing no work at all.... You can't go deeper and know what you're doing the whole time.*
>
> — CLAIRE DEDERER

79. Write a scene in which someone is attempting something for the first time and has no idea what they're doing and is very bad at it. You might try starting with the words "I have never done this before and..."

I sense sometimes I should stop chasing this question, if only for my peace of mind, but it remains for me so utterly elusively a fundamental question: whether a person is shaped most by the iron rails of blood lineage or by the land and the strong and supple hands of experience.

— RICK BASS

80. Write about how your family shaped you. By genes? History? Guilt? Praise? Or maybe they had nothing to do with who you are today. Start with the words "I was shaped by..."

81. Write how the landscape and weather you live in have shaped you. The temperature, the wind, the vast spaces or the cramped streets, or the rows of identical houses. Have you fought the landscape or given in to it?

> *I think the fear of insanity touches everybody who works in the imaginative arts, who is really plunging deeply into themselves. We're like people with one foot nailed to the floor. . . . Danger that if you pull too hard you will indeed float away and the bedrock of reality, which we have been brought up to believe is the only reality, will no longer be valid, and we'll just be crazies.*

> — CLIVE BARKER

82. Write about a time you felt crazy and unhinged. Perhaps with anger or grief or jealousy. Or maybe with being stuck in a situation you couldn't get out of.

83. Write a scene, in dialogue, of someone accusing another of being crazy and the other person denying it.

And it's that transaction, of reaching into your own dream life, your own smartness, your own aliveness, your own knowledge of the world and handing it over to other people — the extraordinary way in which they then give it back to you quadrupled — that becomes an incredible metaphor, not just for art, but for life.

— ALLAN GURGANUS

84. Write about the part of yourself you can hand over to fictional characters. Is it your flaws, your fears? Your knowledge about something specific in the world? Your values?

85. Write about a time you gave something away. Either material or money, or time or knowledge or care. Was it a sacrifice or a relief to give it away?

86. Write about a transaction that made you uncomfortable.

> *Writing is a way to fathom what we have lost, to make sense out of what makes no sense....I don't believe everything happens for a reason, but I have faith in our ability to retrieve from loss something valuable to keep, or to give away.*
>
> — ABIGAIL THOMAS

87. Write about a loss you thought you'd never get over. Maybe it's ongoing, maybe you got over it.

88. Write about where loss goes — where and how loss fits into life, how it can be accepted or not accepted. Maybe this is something one of your characters is going through. Or maybe it's what your memoir is about.

89. Write about a time you lost or broke a material object you loved. Describe the object and its history, the emotions — trivial or huge — that you felt.

> *It takes a long time to learn that nothing is wasted. It takes a long time, and a lot of suffering usually, to understand that there is more to life and to poetry than our conscious purposes.*
>
> — M. C. RICHARDS

90. Write about something you did that you felt was a waste of time but that turned out to be very much worth it. Or vice versa.

91. Write about a conscious purpose. Yours or a character's, large or small.

Mountains are giant, restful, absorbent. You can heave your spirit into a mountain and the mountain will keep it, folded, and not throw it back as some creeks will. The creeks are the world with all it stimulus and beauty; I live there. But the mountains are home.

— ANNIE DILLARD

92. Write about a time in the mountains, real or imagined. If you're writing fiction, you might give a character a memory of a vacation in the mountains.

93. Write about the difference between where you live and home. Or is where you live also home?

This is all that I want to do with my life. *These words arose as if from nowhere in my mind, astonishing me.* This is all that I want to do with my life. *They hit with the force of an inner directive that cannot be questioned. They arose again and again, as if rising on the swells of the music itself.*

— PERRI KNIZE

94. Write about a time when what you wanted to do with your life became clear to you. Or about a time when you couldn't figure out what to do with your life.

95. Write about an obsession.

> *Doesn't a name like an orange*
> *Creep into your heart?*
>
> — PABLO NERUDA

96. Write about a name that creeps into your heart. The name of someone or something you love — an animal, a place, weather, a song.

97. Write about your own name. Who named you this and why? What would your name be if you chose it yourself?

98. Make a list of words that you love. Either words whose sound you love or names of things you love. Don't think; just trust that the right words will come if you get out of the way.

99. Write a paragraph using the list above. Maybe fiction, or maybe something about you and your life.

We have forgotten what rocks, plants, and animals still know. We have forgotten how to be — to be still, to be ourselves, to be where life is: here and now.

— ECKHART TOLLE

100. Write what you notice when you're still. Go outdoors and leave your expectations behind. Look at a rock or a tree or a flower, observe a dog or a cat or a bird. Or a city bus or a tall building. Stay in the here and now. See what words come to you when you're not trying to accomplish something.

In 1976 my glasses were so big I could clean the lenses with a squeegee. Not only were they huge, they were also green with Playboy emblems embossed on the stems. Today these frames sound ridiculous, but back then they were actually quite stylish. Time is cruel to everything but seems to have singled out eyeglasses for special punishment.

— DAVID SEDARIS

101. Write about a pair of glasses, prescription or sunglasses, that you own or once owned. Write about loving your glasses or hating them, how you feel or felt when wearing them.

102. Write about a time you couldn't see. Literally or figuratively.

103. Write about something that time has been cruel to.

> *When you make a metaphor, you call something by a wrong name.... There is always a contradiction. You are not just calling a house a house, but rather a playground, a jungle, a curse, a wound, a paradise.*
>
> — PETER ELBOW

104. Write your own metaphor for the fear — or joy — of writing your first line today. Close your eyes and imagine a landscape (arid desert or lush rain forest?) — or animal or weather or music — that feels close to your emotions. Or a piece of furniture or a sandwich. The great thing about a metaphor is that there are no rules or boundaries; you have to loosen up to write one, and it works or it doesn't. If the fear or joy of writing the first line makes you feel like a barbecue pit, so be it.

105. Write about a gift from a recent visitor. Maybe something you hadn't thought about — a joke they told you, gossip, good conversation. Or a tedious visit that gave you a different kind of gift — an insight into the visitor or yourself, your needs, your judgments.

106. Write about a gift you didn't want.

> *Experience is all we have, and it is only through our bodies that we have it, and only through our senses that we can know and convey it.*
>
> — TRISTINE RAINER

107. Write about a moment experienced through your body. Making love, making breakfast, going to a party, having a fight, an experience you've had or you imagine for your character. Leave out thought and emotion, and let all information be conveyed through the body and senses.

> *I know some things about scars. I know how, as a jagged tear mends, it hurts more ferociously, pulls apart more easily, in the end hardens up more unevenly than a straight cut, say from a tin can or a scalpel.*
>
> — NATALIE KUSZ

108. Write about your own scars, how they happened, where they are on your body.

109. Write about your hidden scars.

To the child, and to the adult who, like Socrates, knows that there is still a child in the wisest of us, fairy tales reveal truths about mankind and oneself.

— BRUNO BETTELHEIM

110. Write yourself as a character in a fairy tale. What is the goal for this character? To escape the tower where he or she has been imprisoned? To become king or queen? To get through the forest in the dark of night?

111. Write about a transformation you once had. Or need to have now.

Suddenly I felt the precise body of your poems beneath
me,
like a raft, *I felt the words as something portable again,*
a cup, a newspaper, a pin.

— NAOMI SHIHAB NYE

112. Write about a raft, real or metaphoric. A raft that one way or another you swam toward. When you reached it, you were able to rest on it or were saved from drowning.

113. Write a poem or a paragraph that could be a raft for your reader. Use your own experiences of deep water and trouble. What would you need and want to hear? Go deep.

114. Write a list of phrases or copy a few lines of a poem that you can carry around with you. Words that will remind you of what you need reminding of, words or phrases that can comfort and inspire you.

Creation, whatever its form, is not an act of will, but an act of faith.

— LLOYD ALEXANDER

115. Write about a time you acted on faith. A time when there was no evidence that what you did would be of value or would work out, but you simply forged on, ignoring the odds.

116. Write about a time you lost faith.

I [write this book] to both admonish and encourage myself. It's also intended as a wake-up call for the motivation that, somewhere along the line, went dormant. I'm writing, in other words, to put my thoughts in some kind of order. And in hindsight — in the final analysis it's always in hindsight — this may very well end up a kind of memoir that centers on the act of running.

— HARUKI MURAKAMI

117. Write yourself a wake-up call for motivation. Write it in your journal — encourage yourself, put your thoughts in order. Or write the opening to an essay about discovering motivation. Or give motivation to a fictional character to think about and act on.

118. Write about an activity that you love. Running, as Murakami wrote about in his memoir, or traveling, playing the piano, teaching, gardening, cooking, rescuing dogs — or anything you do that you feel passionate about. Could a memoir be based on this activity? An essay? Is there a metaphor in it for your life? Could you give this activity to a character in fiction?

In order to do creative work...you must go through long or short spells of not knowing what is going on, of being irritated, and not being able to find the cause, of being willing to work as hard as you can and what happens isn't valuable enough, isn't what you meant to do, what you meant to say. Then you just have to keep on working.

— ELLEN GILCHRIST

119. Write an irritated rant. Write in your journal about being stuck or hitting that wall again, or anything that's currently making you mad. Or let one of your characters get really, really irritated and frustrated about something.

120. Write about a time you didn't know what was going on.

> *To construct compelling characters, make sure they have an understandable purpose, that they're believable... that they inspire empathy, and that they're complex enough to sustain interest. One dependable method of developing complexity is to give your character a recognizable inner conflict.*
>
> — BILLY MERNIT

121. Write about a time you were conflicted and wanted two things at once. What did you want? Did you feel guilty? Frustrated? Sad?

122. Write an interview with yourself, or one of your characters, about a conflict. Try writing a question and then writing the answer with your opposite hand. Or the question with your opposite hand and the answer with the other. Fool around; let yourself be surprised.

Having the faith, endurance or just plain stubbornness to stay committed against all odds is meaningless without love. An artist who doesn't love his or her art can't make a real commitment to it; all the struggles, the blocks, the highs and lows, become merely a test of one's will, or ego.

— DENNIS PALUMBO

123. Write about making a commitment to something because of the overwhelming love you feel for it. Maybe it's a commitment to a person or to an animal. Or maybe it's to books and writing.

124. Write ten reasons — or a hundred — why you can't write what you want to write. Then write ten — or a hundred — reasons why you can.

125. Write a list of what feels too risky to write about. You can write it in code ("that week in 2008") or use initials. Or give a character a list of things he or she won't talk about because it feels too risky.

126. Write a paragraph about one thing on the list above. If you can't write a paragraph, write just one sentence.

When you consider something like death, after which . . .
we may well go out like a candle flame, then it probably
doesn't matter if we try too hard, are awkward some-
times, care for one another too deeply, are excessively
curious about nature, are too open to experience, enjoy
a nonstop expense of the senses in an effort to know life
intimately and lovingly.

— DIANE ACKERMAN

127. Write about a time you loved and cared too much. Did you try too hard? Were there things you did and said that now make you cringe? Or did it all turn out for the best?

128. Write about a time you felt awkward. Write about your hands, your arms, how your feet moved, how your voice sounded.

129. Write about a time you were excessively curious.

Everybody has to have their little tooth of power.
Everyone wants to be able to bite.

— MARY OLIVER

130. Write about a time you wanted and needed power but didn't have it. Over a person, over a situation, or in a job.

131. Write about a time you were bitten. By a bug or an animal — or by desire or curiosity.

I want poetry to be the way it used to come when I was a child. The Muse flew; I flew. Let me return to that child being, and rest from prose.

— MAXINE HONG KINGSTON

132. Write a poem about the book or story you're writing or want to write. Write about the theme, or one scene, or the setting — or a character. Let yourself feel as free and uninhibited as a five-year-old. Make it nonlinear and wild. Fly.

> *To speak, and to write, is to assert who we are, what we think. The necessary other side is to surrender these things — to stand humbled and stunned and silent before the wild and inexplicable beauties and mysteries of being.*
>
> — JANE HIRSHFIELD

133. Write who you are and what you think. Start every line with "I am…" or "I think…"

134. Write about a time you surrendered. Either silent and stunned, or loud and angry.

> *The visual world contains "messages" beneath its apparent disorder, just as meanings lie beneath the apparent disorder of the dream.*
>
> — JOYCE CAROL OATES

135. Write about disorder in a specific place — a room where you live, a closet, a garage, your desk. Write what objects are not in order; write about the mess in physical detail. Try to write specific description, leaving out nonessential adjectives.

136. Write about a time you felt your whole life was in disorder.

> *As a young man my father had been a drapery salesman in a department store, and ever after his hands were at their best when smoothing fabric for display — the left one holding a piece of cloth unrolled from a bolt while the right lovingly eased and teased the wrinkles from it, his fingers spread and their tips lightly touching the cloth as if under them was something grand and alive like the flank of a horse.*
>
> — TED KOOSER

137. Write "My father is/was a man who..." Maybe it's a few paragraphs, maybe a poem with each line starting with those words.

138. Write about your father's hands. Write a description of them working or doing something familiar — shaving, raking leaves, driving a car. Look at your own hands, and write about how they are similar to your father's. Or totally different.

139. Write about a stranger's hands. Next time you're out in public, look at the hands of strangers — serving food or a drink, making change, writing, holding a newspaper, or tapping the keys of a computer. Write about the clues to this person's life you can glean from his or her hands.

At Rachel's memorial service I had been unable to shed a tear, but at the Hollywood Bowl it finally happened....I couldn't stop crying. I covered my face with my hands while the rest of the audience left...and I kept my hands there as Jessica and I walked to the parking lot. I handed the keys over to her and cried all the way home as she drove. I cried as I undressed and cried until I fell asleep. The next morning, when I woke up, I felt better. But I didn't want to talk about what had happened or even think about it.

— MARK SALZMAN

140. Write about a time when you cried uncontrollably. Perhaps it was after the fact, in a surprising place or circumstance. Or write about a time you couldn't cry.

> *There is a Japanese word for things made more beautiful by use, that bear the evidence of their own making, or the individuating marks of time's passage: a kind of beauty not immune to time but embedded in it.*
>
> — MARK DOTY

141. Write about an old and much-used object that you own. Has it become more beautiful with age, or simply old and used? Does it have a history? Try giving the object to one of your characters if you're writing fiction.

142. Write about an object that you've imagined or something you wanted but never possessed. Give the object to a fictional character and let him or her tell you where it came from and how they feel about it. Is it treasure or trash?

> *One of the striking facts of most lives is the recurrence of threads of continuity, the re-echoing of earlier themes, even across deep rifts of change, but when you watch people damaged by their dependence on continuity, you wonder about the nature of commitment, about the need for a new and more fluid way to imagine the future.*
>
> — MARY CATHERINE BATESON

143. Write about the threads of continuity in your life. Or write about cutting the threads and reinventing your life.

144. Write about a deep rift of change you've gone through. Was it a change in spite of you? Or one that you created?

145. Write about a time there was damage from not changing — stuckness, or boredom, or lost chances.

> *The relationship between commitment and doubt is by no means an antagonistic one. Commitment is healthiest when it is not without doubt, but in spite of doubt.*
>
> — ROLLO MAY

146. Write about the doubt you had when you made a specific commitment — to a relationship or to accomplishing something.

These nine characters turn up from time to time — not because they're from my family, but because they represent all families, the people we have to deal with when we think about pursuing our dreams without making the lives of our friends and family — and our own — a living hell.

— CAROLYN SEE

147. Write one line about each of the nine — or the three or five or twelve — main characters in your life. Your family, your friends, the people you see or talk to every day who are part of your life and history.

148. Write about the people who support your dreams. And the specific ways they encourage you.

149. Write about the negative characters who can make life a living hell. Do a little venting in your journal about anyone in your life who falls into this category.

> *You can observe a lot by watching. Yogi Berra said that, and it's true. Go outside and observe a street scene. Pick out a man and woman together.*
>
> — TWYLA THARP

150. Write down everything you see a couple in public doing. If one scratches his chin, if the other touches his arm, if they sip coffee, if one checks a cell phone — write it all down until you have twenty items on your list.

151. Write an idea for a short story from the list you've made. From their actions and posture, can you tell something about the couple's relationship? Are they long married? On a first date? Old friends or siblings? Ex-spouses?

152. Write down what another couple is doing in public, but only list the actions that you find interesting. This one can be an example of how you judge what you see and your own writing, your need to write *interesting* stuff, so the list might be shorter but not necessarily better.

(These exercises are adapted from Twyla Tharp's book *The Creative Habit*.)

> *What is this, my sister asks again.*
> *It's an explanation, I answer.*
> *An explanation?*
> *It's an apology, I say.*
> *An apology?*
> *It's a present, I say.*

— ABIGAIL THOMAS

153. Write a scene in six lines of dialogue. Have a character give a present or ask a question. Or write six lines about a time you gave someone a present.

154. Write about an apology that failed.

155. Write a scene in which someone is constantly explaining something.

> *We don't tell ourselves, "I'm never going to write my symphony." Instead we say, "I am going to write my symphony; I'm just going to start tomorrow."*
>
> — STEVEN PRESSFIELD

156. Write about what you're going to start tomorrow. Or next week. Or when the weather gets better, there's more money, you have more time, or you're in the mood.

157. Write about what you're going to start today. Even if you're not ready or inspired, or you don't have the time, write the side door into your story — just one idea. One word, one sentence, one paragraph; that's all you have to write.

158. Write about a time you procrastinated until you lost what you wanted or needed.

The way you get to this unconscious place is by writing every day. Or not even writing. Some days you may be rewriting, rereading, or just sitting there scrolling back and forth through the text. This is enough to bring you back into the dream of your story.... What, you ask, is the dream of your story? This is a mood and a continent of thought below your conscious mind.

— WALTER MOSLEY

159. Write about the dream of your story in your journal. On the days you feel stuck or rushed or it's impossible for some reason to write, just jot down notes, random thoughts about your story. Stay connected to your story in any way possible so that your subconscious will continue to work on it.

160. Write about socks. White socks, patterned socks, kneesocks, black socks. Folding them, wearing them, knitting them, buying them, putting them in a drawer. Or no socks, never wearing socks. If you're writing fiction, give your character a pair of socks, or write about a memory of socks from your childhood.

161. Write a list of ordinary things that are part of your life and therefore part of your story. Write a riff on soap, on toothbrushes, on soup, on TV clickers, on kitty litter, or baseball caps, or whatever *stuff* is in your story. From your point of view or your character's.

> *When I least expect it something strikes me. Just now, for instance, we were driving westward and stopped at the West Virginia welcome station, and I looked at the woman next to me who tucked her purse between her legs to wash her hands, and that little action triggered something in me — I suddenly thought of all the things we do subconsciously to keep things neat, and the way women carry purses around.*
>
> — RITA DOVE

162. Write about someone carrying a purse. How they carry it, or where they put it when entering a room.

163. Write about the contents of a purse or a briefcase. Your own or that of a character. Are there shopping lists in the purse? Saved fortune-cookie slips? Gum, loose change, keys, condoms, combs, glasses, cigarettes? Are there papers or just a computer in the briefcase? A sandwich, a clean shirt? One way a reader gets to know us, or our characters, is by the things we or they carry.

164. Write about an action that someone takes to keep neat and clean. Maybe something you do but never consciously thought about before.

165. Write a scene in which someone tidies up a room. Be specific about the things they put away or throw away. Why are they cleaning up the room? What are they thinking or talking about as they do it?

> *As a young teenager I looked desperately for things to read that might excuse me or assure me I wasn't the only one, that might confirm an identity I was unhappily piecing together.*
>
> — EDMUND WHITE

166. Write about what you were searching for as a teenager. A book, a story, or a friend who could tell you that you weren't strange or boring or some kind of freak. Someone or something that would confirm who you really were.

167. Write about your best friend as a teenager. Or about having no friends. Or write about a whole pack of pals.

> *Maybe it started with my incapacities and failures.... Maybe it was power I was after.... The hard part was figuring out which things to say. I tried writing stories. All the people in them were doomed.*
>
> — WILLIAM KITTREDGE

168. Write about a specific failure. Either a small failure — a dinner that went up in smoke — or a life-altering failure like a divorce or lost job.

169. Write about being blamed or blaming someone for a failure. Maybe the blame dead-ends in anger, or maybe it turns into acceptance or forgiveness.

170. Write about a person, or an event or plan, that is doomed. Maybe a character in fiction — someone who can't ever change or adjust. Or the event or plan that a character is betting on to make everything different.

> *The pitcher cries for water to carry*
> *and a person for work that is real.*
>
> — MARGE PIERCY

171. Write about a time when work felt real to you, necessary and satisfying. Paid or unpaid, professional or domestic, physical or mental.

Go forth and be fancy today.

— RACHEL KANN

172. Write the first image that pops into your head from the quote above. Don't overthink it. Don't think at all. Just jump in. Be fancy and go forth and write about it.

> *Writing in that state is the most profound satisfaction
> she knows, but her access to it comes and goes without
> warning. She may pick up her pen and follow it with
> her hand as it moves across the paper; she may pick up
> her pen and find that she's merely herself, a woman in
> a housecoat holding a pen, afraid and uncertain, only
> mildly competent, with no idea about where to begin or
> what to write....She picks up her pen.*
>
> — MICHAEL CUNNINGHAM

173. Write about picking up a pen. Write about something you or your character wrote that was urgent, or a note, a shopping list, an entry in a journal, a check.

When I stopped resisting, when I stopped trying to change, when I trusted that there was nothing missing inside, that I didn't have to choose between one part of me over another, I rediscovered me.

— SUE BENDER

174. Write about a time when you stopped resisting. Write about what you were resisting, what made you stop, how you felt when you did.

175. Write a scene in which a character is resisting something. Start the scene with dialogue: "No, I won't..."

> *I exhort, I interfere. I'm impatient. For God's sake, it isn't that hard to live. One of the pieces of advice I give is: Don't suffer future pain.*
>
> — SUSAN SONTAG

176. Write about a time you interfered, your impatience. And what you said. Or did.

177. Write about the best advice you ever got.

Coming from a family where literary tradition runs largely to the picture postcard, it is not surprising that I have never really succeeded in explaining to my grandmother exactly what it is that I do. It is not that my grandmother is unintelligent; quite the contrary. It is simply that so firmly implanted are her roots in retail furniture that she cannot help but view all other occupations from this rather limited vantage point.

— FRAN LEBOWITZ

178. Write what you know about your grandmother's life. What does/did she think of you? Where are her roots? What stories did she tell you when you were little? How are/were her perspectives limited by her experience?

179. Write about a time someone thought you were dressed inappropriately. Did you know from their expression, or did they tell you in words?

180. Write about a time you felt you were dressed inappropriately. What were you wearing? Where were you? How did you realize it was inappropriate? Did anyone else even notice?

181. Write a scene in which someone appears at a strange time and place wearing a nightgown.

> *Work with all your intelligence and love. Work freely and rollickingly as though you were talking to a friend who loves you. Mentally (at least three or four times a day) thumb your nose at all know-it-alls, jeerers, critics, doubters.*
>
> — BRENDA UELAND

182. Write about knowing that a friend loves you. Write about specific actions and words that make you know you're loved.

183. Write about thumbing your nose at someone or something. Write why they or it deserves this.

> *All good writing is* swimming under water *and holding your breath.*
>
> — F. Scott Fitzgerald

184. Write about a time you held your breath. Underwater or not.

One night they both needed different things
of a similar kind; she, solace; he, to be consoled.

— STEPHEN DUNN

185. Write about a time that you needed to be consoled. Write about a time you tried to console someone. Write about finding solace.

186. Write about needing different things than your partner or friend needs. What does he or she always want? What do you always want?

187. Write about how it feels for you when you write.
     Write how you think it should feel.

188. Write about your other job. Office worker, hair-
     dresser, musician, doctor, janitor, lawyer, or what-
     ever it may be. Write the details of your work
     that you take for granted, something most people
     wouldn't know or think about. Write how you
     feel about your job.

189. Write five images about money. Choose an image
     that has trouble in it, and write. (This exercise is
     adapted from Lynda Barry.)

My vocation is to write stories — invented things or things which I can remember from my own life, but in any case stories, things that are concerned only with memory and imagination and have nothing to do with erudition. This is my vocation and I shall work at it till I die.

— Natalia Ginzburg

190. Write five things you remember, starting each line with "I remember..." Choose the one you don't want to write about, and write about it. How old are you in the memory? What's the weather like? Where are you living?

191. Write about what you want to do until you die.

> *The two most engaging powers of an author are to make new things familiar, and familiar things new.*
>
> — SAMUEL JOHNSON

192. Write a short list of things — objects — so familiar that you never think about them. Choose one, and write about it as if you've never seen it before.

193. Write a familiar action that you do daily that has something to do with where you live. Taking a subway, saddling up a horse, shoveling snow, running in the sand — activities that depend on location and/or weather. Something you do that is so familiar you never pay attention to it.

> *Every human event happens somewhere, and the reader wants to know what that "somewhere" was like.*
>
> — WILLIAM ZINSSER

194. Write the details of where you live now. What people wear on the streets, where they buy food and shop and watch movies or sports, what's trendy in your town or unchanged since the eighties. Remember that your reader loves to learn about new places but also loves to read the familiar details of home.

> *I've found that any day's routine interruptions and distractions don't much hurt a work in progress and may actually help it in some ways. It is, after all, the dab of grit that seeps into an oyster's shell that makes the pearl, not pearl-making seminars with other oysters.*
>
> — STEPHEN KING

195. Write all the grit that's getting into your shell today as you're trying to work. The noises, the errands to run, the need to cook or clean, the car problems — let it all out on paper. Maybe some of it can turn into a pearl.

> *Two or three things I know, two or three things I know for sure, and one of them is that if we are not beautiful to each other, we cannot know beauty in any form.*
>
> — DOROTHY ALLISON

196. Write two or three things you know. Don't overthink this.

197. Write two or three things you know for sure. Again, don't overthink. Just write.

198. Write about a time you felt beautiful to someone else. Or not.

> *Story, the kind we tell around campfires to comfort our-*
> *selves, the kind we tell as parables to warn each other,*
> *the kind we tell to save ourselves.*
>
> — ZZ PACKER

199. Write about a time you were comforted or saved by a story. Start with "When…"

200. Write about a time you warned someone. Was the danger another person, an action, a desire, or something else?

Secretly writers do love the censor within. We say we hate that sanctimonious inner voice, but there is no better excuse for procrastination, lethargy and despair....Writer, beware! The inner critic is insidious, subversive, always available for depressive episodes. Stay alert. Know the enemy. Know yourself.

— ALLEGRA GOODMAN

201. Write down what your inner critic/censor is saying to you. Then, if possible, find the humor in it. Write back a calm reply, and move on to the next exercise.

> *This is what separates artists from ordinary people: the belief, deep in our hearts, that if we build our castles well enough, somehow the ocean won't wash them away. I think this is a wonderful kind of person to be.*
>
> — ANNE LAMOTT

202. Write about building your castle — how sturdy it is, how well made it is, and how it's constructed with love and faith. Call it a castle or a fort, a deep well or a boat, any metaphor you wish.

I want to describe the Salinas Valley in detail but in sparse detail so that there can be a real feeling of it. It should be sights and sounds, smells and colors but put down with simplicity.

— JOHN STEINBECK

203. Write the sights and sounds, smells and colors of your story. How many specific details can you come up with? How many nonessential adjectives can you get rid of? Or write about the place you're in now.

> *A good portion of our lives is gladly casual, and happily ordinary. The other dark and lustrous place is not casual. It is not ordinary. Neither does it pertain so much to the particularities of our lives as to the commonality of our lives.*
>
> — MARY OLIVER

204. Write a quick scene from the casual, ordinary part of your life. Maybe dinner with a friend or family, or waking up in the morning with someone you live with.

205. Write a scene from the other place in your life or your fictional character's life. The dark and lustrous place, or maybe simply dark — 3:00 AM anxiety.

> *There is no place to put this experience, no folder in the mental hard drive that says "catastrophe." It is not something you want to remember, not something you want to forget.*
>
> — A.M. HOMES

206. Write about something that you don't want to remember but don't want to forget.

207. Write about the moment you heard of a shared catastrophe — 9/11 or an assassination, something you observed from the distance of television. What were you doing when you found out? Who did you call or who called you?

Finding the words — or receiving the words, let's say — is a matter of jumpstarting the quiet machinery of dreams while in a fully waking state.

— STEVEN HEIGHTON

208. Write about a recent dream you had. If you can't remember your dreams, keep a notebook next to your bed, and start jotting down any images you remember when you first wake up.

209. Write a poem using the images from a dream. Don't worry if it doesn't connect or make sense.

210. Write about a time you felt lonely and freakish. Was it a specific moment, or was it a whole period of your life?

211. Write about something you read or heard or somehow discovered that made you feel less lonely, less freakish.

You cannot play Goodnight Moon. You cannot bid farewell to the yellow house on the corner. You cannot duck inside the church and light a candle. You cannot stop and get coffee. You can only look straight ahead and drive. You can only think about the next thing, the hello and not the goodbye, the up and onward and not the over and out.

— MEGHAN DAUM

212. Write about a time you looked straight ahead and drove away, or walked or ran away.

213. Write about a time you played Goodnight Moon as you left. The rooms and the house, the things, and the places you said good-bye to.

> *This book begins with an old proverb, "When God wishes to rejoice the heart of a poor man, He makes him lose his donkey and find it again." In the summer of 1998, I lost the donkey upon which I had ridden for many years, the ability to write. It was something that had given meaning to my life for forty years, and it was gone.*
>
> — TED KOOSER

214. Write about your own donkey, something you lost and then found again. Did you find it in a new shape, another life, a different gift?

215. Write about what gives meaning to your life. For the past year or five, ten, or forty years — why and how has an occupation or belief or person or cause given meaning to your life?

Artistically, I don't find my own life compelling mate-
rial — all those boyfriends, all that angst. It seems like
the same script over and over again. Yet if there was a
way to get beneath the surface and redeem it, make it
stand for something more, I would. Perhaps I am too
blind or proud to use what is there.

— PHYLLIS THEROUX

216. Write about one of those boyfriends or girlfriends,
and the angst. Write the names and places and
what you did or didn't do.

217. Write about a time you were too proud or too
blind. Write about the consequences.

> *Looking at an old family photograph when I was twelve,*
> *I saw a face I didn't recognize. Asking who this was, I*
> *first heard her story. Suicides have a way of haunting*
> *the next generation, and adolescence is when most of us*
> *begin to know who we will be. I believe I became a writer*
> *in order to tell her story and possibly redeem it.*
>
> — KATHLEEN NORRIS

218. Write about your first encounter with death. The death of someone you knew when you were young — a grandparent, a friend of your parents, your own friend. Write how you were told about it. Write what words were used.

219. Write about a suicide or the accidental death of someone you knew. Write about how you found out, the first thing you did, who you called.

220. Write about a specific funeral you once attended. Write the images and details you can remember.

221. Write about someone who almost died but didn't.

222. Write about a family photograph. What doesn't the picture show?

I'm writing out of desperation. I felt compelled to write to make sense of it myself — so I don't end up saying peculiar things like "I'm black and I'm proud." I write so I don't end up as a set of slogans and clichés.

— JAMAICA KINCAID

223. Write about a time you did something out of desperation. Write about how your heart felt, your mouth, your hands. What was at stake?

224. Write a cliché or slogan you've used over and over. Something that's become meaningless because you've said it so much.

225. Write about what's behind the cliché. What you or a character really means, what you're trying to say.

> *Well — there I got that premise down in dialogue. And since this is one of the very most important things in the book, it is my hope that it comes over clearly. This must be remembered because on this rests a large part of my structure of the book.*
>
> — JOHN STEINBECK

226. Write a dialogue between two of your main characters. Have them tell each other what they need and want and what's in the way.

227. Write a dialogue with yourself about the reason you're writing your memoir or essay or novel. Ask hard questions. Write the premise of your book.

> *Over the years, the story of my parents' courtship and marriage has acquired a delicacy that has kept me at a distance, like an ancient hand-blown piece of glass that might disintegrate if I got too close.*
>
> — DANI SHAPIRO

228. Write what you know of your parents' courtship. Is there one common story, or are there two versions? Or more? Or no stories?

229. Write what you know about your parents' marriage. Or what you don't know. Write a reoccurring dialogue between them, the praise and/or the put-downs.

What was happening was happening to us both. I believe it is always so, mutual and, at least at first, equally intense, if it is genuine inloveness. The actual thing — inloveness — requires something like a spark leaping back and forth from one to the other, becoming more intense every moment.

— SHELDON VANAUKEN

230. Write about a time when the sparks started to leap back and forth. Between you and someone else or between your characters.

231. Write about what you want when you fall in love with someone. Write about what you need. Write about what you get.

232. Write about a time the sparks only went in one direction.

> *But what can you say about the first woman in your life? She was Mum. She sorted me out. She fed me. She was forever slicking my hair and straightening my clothes in public. Humiliation. But it's Mum. I didn't realize until later that she was also my mate. She could make me laugh. There was music all the time, and I do miss her so.*
>
> — KEITH RICHARDS

233. Write about your mother, your mom, your mama, your mum, whoever reared you. What can you say about her? Make a list of things she did that may have humiliated or annoyed you, or not.

234. Write something you realized as an adult about the person who reared you. Something you didn't understand as a child.

I can still smell the odor that came out of the trunk when we'd crowbarred the padlock off and opened it. The smell had seeped into the letters and endures there — damp paper, and gun oil, and chalk from the edges of a puzzling cedar box, which we eventually figured out was a turkey call.

— MARY KARR

235. Write what you smelled when you opened an old trunk — or an attic door or a storage unit or house — that had been closed up for a long time. Old trunks, wood fires, perfume, wind-dried sheets — every odor carries a memory.

236. Write about what you once found in a trunk or storage box or attic. Write about old letters and photographs, or things whose use or origin puzzled you.

Actions just are. You cry; a shoulder is there. You laugh; other laughter joins you. You feel cold in the night; an arm wraps around your waist and pulls you into the warmth of his sleeping body. Only through this, the most trusted form of knowing.

— SAMANTHA DUNN

237. Write about an ordinary action someone takes to comfort you.

238. Write about being cold in bed at night. Or being too hot. In either case, what action did you take?

Among the few consolations of what has been called writer's block is the assurance that, so long as one has it, one is, indeed, a writer. Of course, the longer it goes the more it resembles, and risks being mistaken for, proctologist's block, real estate agent's block, and other obstructions ordinaire.

— THOMAS LYNCH

239. Write about having a block of another kind, other than writer's block. Maybe an exercise or travel block, or agoraphobia or some kind of obstruction or phobia connected to your day job or personal life.

We survive, and we blend right back into the crowd, and we don't know from day to day whether we'll be alive tomorrow, but at least if we get out there and tell our stories and call ourselves survivors, we know that we're alive today.

— JENNIE NASH

240. Write about a time you survived. A time when you got through a serious illness or an accident, a divorce, a death, or any trauma that turned your world upside down.

241. Write about blending into a crowd. Either with a crowd of people who have gone through the same thing or an ordinary crowd who knows nothing of what you've been through.

242. Write about a time you triumphed over something really hard.

Knowing something is one thing. Knowing how to use that knowing is another. Knowing how to use that knowing selflessly is wisdom. Wisdom is the application of knowledge with love.

— PETER DUNNE

243. Write about something you know how to do or know about. Anything at all that you know a lot about or that you're good at doing.

244. Write how you use this thing you know or can do.

> *I answered that what I wanted more than anything else in the world was to write, nothing else but that, nothing....No answer, just a quick glance immediately averted, a slight shrug, unforgettable.*
>
> — MARGUERITE DURAS

245. Write what you wanted/want more than anything else in the world.

246. Write the reaction of someone close to you when you told them about it. Or write about a time when you were cautious or afraid or embarrassed to tell anyone what you wanted most.

The people who come to see us bring us their stories. They hope they tell them well enough so that we understand the truth of their lives. They hope we know how to interpret their stories correctly. We have to remember that what we hear is their story.

— ROBERT COLES

247. Write someone else's story, that of a friend or someone you once sat next to on a plane. Include the questions you wished you had asked and details you'd like to know but didn't ask or forgot to ask.

248. Write a monologue of a fictional character telling you his or her story. Using the first person, have your characters, major or minor, tell you their stories as if they're sitting next to you on a plane.

So married life began. And the joys of solitude. No contradiction was involved. The one went perfectly with the other. To feel oneself held and cherished and accompanied, and yet to be alone. To be closely and physically entwined, and yet feel solitude's friendly presence, as warm and undesolating as contiguity itself.

— JOHN BAYLEY

249. Write about a time you were able to find solitude in a close relationship.

250. Write about the closest relationship you've ever had.

251. Write about a time you felt lonely in a close relationship.

When I pull the letter from the mailbox, my heart starts jackhammering. I return to my second-floor Leimert Park apartment, leaping two white stairs per stride. Sit down at the heavy wooden desk. Tight-fist the letter opener butcher knife–style to steady my trembling hand.

— MICHAEL DATCHER

252. Write a scene in which a character pulls a letter from a mailbox or opens an email, heart jackhammering. What's at stake here for your character? What is your character waiting for, hoping for? Or dreading?

253. Write about receiving a letter or email when your own heart pounded at the sight of the return address. Who was it from, and what was at stake?

> *There is a gap in understanding between me and our friends and acquaintances. I can't quite understand a life without books and study and music and pictures and a driving passion. And they, on the other hand, can't understand why I have to write, why I'm a writer.*
>
> — MADELEINE L'ENGLE

254. Write about a time you felt a gap in understanding. What did someone close to you need that you didn't? And vice versa.

255. Write three things that you can't imagine living without. (Taking for granted basic needs.)

I'm suffering from acute nervous laziness — the kind which is caused by having too much to do. Also, the weather is tropically steamy. The ocean yesterday was so strange, shining silver and quite smooth and streamy, like a vast river. Went down on the beach today; horrible, dirty, crowded and the water full of rocks.

— CHRISTOPHER ISHERWOOD

256. Write about a time when your mood and the weather and your surroundings connected in some way. Or maybe the opposite occurred.

257. Write about a time you had too much to do.

> *At a desk, in front of a computer, my mind goes blank, but as soon as I take off (to the supermarket, to Australia), inspiration strikes. Journeys are the midwives of books.*
>
> — ALAIN DE BOTTON

258. Write about a recent journey you took, far away or closer to home. Did it inspire you in any way? Did you take notes?

259. Write about a journey you're dreaming of taking. What are your expectations?

260. Write about a trip to the supermarket as if it's a journey to a foreign country. Pay attention to the details you usually ignore; treat every aisle as an exotic destination.

It seems like they're holding two things in their hands at once — something that's fragile and something that's burning. And that's a very hard thing to do. You've got to be spiritually there and intellectually there.

— BETH HENLEY

261. Write about a moment when a character feels as if he or she is holding something fragile in one hand and in the other hand something that's burning. What's the conflict? What is he or she trying to explain, or to keep secret or safe?

262. Write a scene in which you or a character is present emotionally but not intellectually. Or vice versa.

> *A major character [in a book] has a mission in life, based on a major ambition or motivation, and expressed through a simple combination of the* major *human emotions.*
>
> — KENNETH ATCHITY

263. Write a monologue for your protagonist, stating his or her mission in life. What's the motivation for this mission? Consider how this might be different from, or even at odds with, need and want. If you're writing a memoir, what was your driving motivation during the period in your life that you're writing about? And were you fully aware of it?

264. Write about the emotions that this mission brings out. Are the emotions contradictory?

> *My ageing was very sudden. I saw it spread over my features one by one, changing the relationship between them, making the eyes larger, the expression sadder, the mouth more final, leaving great creases in the forehead. But instead of being dismayed I watched this process with the same sort of interest I might have taken in the reading of a book.*
>
> — MARGUERITE DURAS

265. Write about a time you looked in the mirror and thought you looked older. Write about how you felt — dismayed, sad, or resigned.

266. Write about a time you looked in the mirror and really liked what you saw.

267. Write a scene in which your character looks in the mirror and makes a decision.

> *A strangely warm wind smelling of ozone and clean rain*
> *(though no rain was in sight) eddied around them and*
> *disturbed Jack with its promise of elsewhere.*
>
> — EDMUND WHITE

268. Write about a moment when the weather and/or
     a smell held a memory of another time and place.

> *The dry twigs left of a vanished life, whatever its fullness once was, are rubbed together until they catch fire. Until they make something. Until they make a story.*
>
> — PATRICIA HAMPL

269. Write a few details and highlights, the dry twigs, of the life of someone you knew, a friend or family member who is gone. See if the details can spark into a story.

> *I should fictionalize it more, I should conceal myself, I should consider the responsibilities of characterization, I should conflate her two children into one, or reverse their genders, or otherwise alter them, I should make her boyfriend a husband...I should novelize the whole thing.*
>
> — RICK MOODY

270. Write about a time you felt you revealed too much. Either on paper or in real life.

271. Write a list of "shoulds" for whatever you're writing. And then maybe tear it up.

Recently someone asked about my worst fears — what were they? I couldn't come up with anything. To have a fear you have to be able to imagine the future, and I never think about the future anymore. It is no longer my destination.

— ABIGAIL THOMAS

272. Write your worst fears. Either as a list or just one huge fear. Or if you fear nothing, write about that.

273. Write how you picture your destination in life. Literally, as a place or position, or emotionally and spiritually.

> *From the summer of my twelfth year I carry a series of images more vivid and lasting than any others of my boyhood and indelible beyond all attempts the years make to erase or fade them.*
>
> — LARRY WATSON

274. Write an indelible image from the summer you were twelve years old. Or if there are many images, write them all down. Or if there's another year of your childhood more vivid, write an indelible image from that summer.

275. Write an image you have tried to erase from your memory.

No other word will do. For that's what it was. Gravy.
Gravy, these past ten years.

— RAYMOND CARVER

276. Write about the gravy in your life. Or is there another word for it?

277. Write about the time in the past decade when you felt happiest.

> *When I order food, I always ask how they will prepare it. If I am getting takeout, I ask for the fries to be separate, because I don't like mushy fries. It is my clumsy way of explaining myself, I suppose. A need to define myself as something, the sort of person who prefers her fries to be crisp. If I was always this way or if I'm just controlling what I can during the cancer, I don't remember.*
>
> — CAROLE RADZIWILL

278. Write about a time you tried to stay calm or sane by controlling something ordinary. How the french fries were fixed, what channel to watch on TV, what route to take, or whatever you latched onto for a sense of control.

279. Write about a time when you couldn't control anything.

We fight. The spilled coffee, the shrunken sweater, the oddly made bed, the wrong word, don't criticize me, don't blame me, you resent me, you're doing it wrong. I can't stand this; *we fight and fight. Nothing is too small for us. Anything will do, any tiny trigger sets off a shouting match of blame and accusation.*

— MARYA HORNBACHER

280. Write about a fight over something trivial to cover the real cause of your anger.

281. Write about what was not being fought about because it was too scary. You didn't want to rock the boat or feared the cost of the truth would be too high.

> *What are this person's routines, beliefs? What little things would your characters write in their journals: I ate this, I hate that, I did this, I took the dog for a long walk, I chatted with my neighbor.*
>
> — ANNE LAMOTT

282. Write a page of your character's journal. Include what he or she ate, and feelings about other people and places.

283. Write "I believe" in your own journal and keep going. If you get stuck, start every line with the words "I believe."

284. Write out your own routine, your daily schedule, in your journal. Even though you might think it deadly dull now, in a few years you'll find it fascinating.

I don't know if I ever saw gramma smile. She didn't have anything nice or pretty around the house. The linoleum was so wore off it looked like tar paper on the floor.... On the windows, she had shear lace curtains — they were plastic. Her quilts were all heavy and dark — made from cut up old men's trousers and coats.

— LINDA ST. JOHN

285. Write about an older relative's house. What covers/covered the floors, the windows, the beds?

286. Write about the smiles of two or three people close to you. Or their nonsmiling faces.

It became one of the sharper pleasures of writing memoir: how uncanny to go back in memory to a house from which time has stolen all the furniture, and to find the one remembered chair, and to write it so large, so deep, that it furnishes the entire vacant room. The past comes streaming back on words, and delivers the goods it had absconded with.

— PATRICIA HAMPL

287. Write about a chair from your past. Write a description, the smell and feel of it. Where in the house was the chair? Did you read in it, watch TV?

288. Write about your character's favorite chair from childhood.

*Suddenly there was in the air a rich sense of crisis —
real crisis, yet one that also contained echoes of ideas
like the crisis of language, the crisis of literature, or of
personality. It seemed to me that my existence, whatever I thought, felt, or did, had taken on a kind of
meter, as in poetry or in taxis. . . . I had been given a real
deadline at last.*

— ANATOLE BROYARD

289. Write about a time when you went through a crisis. Of health or relationship or work or finances.
Did you turn toward the crisis or away from it?

290. Write about a deadline that came with the crisis.
Was the clock ticking? A taxi meter? A deadline
for work? The days and months of a life?

> *Most people are conditioned for failure — except, for instance, astronauts. Astronauts are used to success. They come from small, homogeneous towns where they were the captains of the football teams. Start feeling successful and if you are, don't think it was an accident.*
>
> — GORDON LISH

291. Write about a time you felt successful.

292. Write a list of images that you equate with success. What does success mean to you or your characters?

293. Write a list of images of yourself being successful at what you want most, in very concrete ways, real or imagined. Carry those images around in your head for as long as possible.

The new bed is huge. King-size, made of cherry, ordered from a lifestyle catalogue. The cost? I don't care how much it cost, I was tired of a small bed. I was fucking tired of it. The mattresses, also huge, came from DIAL-A-MATTRES ("Leave off the last s for savings!").

— COLIN HARRISON

294. Write about a time when you bought a new bed. Why did you buy it and from where? Write about getting rid of the old bed.

295. Write a scene in which a character's reaction to a current ad or television commercial moves the action.

> *In the grand view, I see gardening as a ritual drama, in which the whole cycle of death and rebirth is enacted annually. But that doesn't prevent me from undertaking the most lowly tasks and truly enjoying them, even weeding and grubbing.... The making of a garden requires the same kind of ruthlessness as the making of a poem.*
>
> — STANLEY KUNITZ

296. Write about your garden or one that you or someone in your family once planted. Or write about never having a garden and why.

297. Write about a time you were ruthless. With a garden, a poem, a relationship, or a place.

> *Writing is how I hear my own voice confronting me, saying that you're trying to excuse yourself with all these explanations — you're trying to say, "It's my family. It's history. It's race," when you know it's actually your own nature. It's who you are — your own nature.*
>
> — DAVID MURA

298. Write a list of excuses you've made for yourself over the years.

299. Write the "why" behind the excuses. Why didn't you, or a character, show up? Why did you take another drink, another piece of cake, the cigarette? Why isn't she talking to you? Why did he get so mad? Why didn't you take the chance, the offer, the good bet?

The town was filled with bars. You could tell each decade from the signs, deco red neon, old-west-style horses and cowboys. What there was to do was beer and rivers. What there was to do was drive. The downtown parking spaces were huge, and when the light changed at the empty corner the people (who were waiting) *walked across in no hurry.*

— SUSANNA SONNENBERG

300. Write what your village/town/city is filled with. Bars, churches, department stores, boutiques? What do people do here? How do they cross the street?

> *There are corruptions inherent in every profession, and to leap (or retreat) into "meaning" is one of the corruptions of mine. For it is no small crime to cram a moment with meaning as a substitute for experiencing that moment. I didn't know that most writing is just an attempt to control the unpredictable reverberations of an experience — to put a stamp on it, own it in some way, and then (not incidentally) sell it.*
>
> — MICHAEL VENTURA

301. Write about a time you controlled something by writing about it.

302. Write about a time you crammed more meaning into a moment than the situation warranted.

No other fear, not even that of ridicule, prevents me from writing these lines which I am willing to risk will be published. Why should I stop my hand from gliding over this paper to which for so many years I've confided what I know about myself, what I've tried to hide, what I've invented and what I've guessed.

— COLETTE

303. Write about a time when you were prevented from doing something because of your fear of ridicule. Write about the worst thing that could have happened. Write about the regret or the relief of not doing it.

304. Write about a time when you tried to hide. A time you invented lies or were silent.

> *I have saved the sense of touch as the last pleasure to be extolled. I wish for the slick feel of silk underclothes and the pinch of sand in my beach shoes. I welcome the sun strong on my back and the tender pelting of snow on my face. Good clothes that fit snugly and strong fearless hands that caress without pain. I want the crunch of hazelnuts between my teeth and ice cream melting on my tongue.*
>
> — MAYA ANGELOU

305. Write about how your clothes feel on your body at this moment. Where cloth or leather touches your skin, how does it feel? What feels tight, what feels good on your body?

306. Write about eating an ice cream cone the next time you have one. Write about the cold on your tongue, how it melts, how it tastes. Pay attention.

307. Write about how the weather feels on your skin. Go outside, and write about how the cold, or rain, or sun feels on your face or your hands.

308. Write about a caress, a touch. Given or received, fearless or fearful.

> *"I suppose there are millions of us this very moment in just the same pain," I tapped on the keys. "Why do I feel so singular?"... Yes, millions of us keeping bedside vigils... each of us trapped in this profound and irrational solitude.*
>
> — NANCY MAIRS

309. Write about a time you were trapped in a profound solitude. Write about feeling singular, as if no one else in the world was going through this.

310. Write about a bedside vigil you once kept. What did your five senses pick up? How did you spend the time? Write about the person who was in the bed.

The problem is not that you can't write but that there is nothing to say. Say well. Say right. Write.

— ANNA MOSCHOVAKIS

311. Write about a time you had nothing to say. You wanted to write but felt that you had nothing to say.

312. Write about a time you couldn't write because what you wanted to write, you couldn't write well. Write about what "wrong" writing would be.

> *The creation of an authentic work of art, the creation of an authentic life — they are one and the same. Neither can be accomplished as long as affectation obstructs the way. The life that lives behind a mask, that calls attention to itself, is doomed to fail.*
>
> — RICHARD BODE

313. Write about a mask you once wore. Or the mask that one of your characters wears. What does the mask represent, and what is it covering up?

314. Write your idea of an authentic life. What part does your writing play in it?

Don't fret too much about noodles. Whatever you do to them, they remain noodle-like, which Providence probably intended.

— PEG BRACKEN

315. Write about a time you cooked noodles, or something else, and did indeed fret. Was it about the meal you were cooking or something else?

316. Write a scene in which your character is cooking noodles. Maybe the noodles become a metaphor for what your character is talking about. Or maybe a focus on cooking pasta becomes a way to avoid joining in the conversation.

> *If you were a member of Jesse James' band and people asked you what you were, you wouldn't say, "Well, I'm a desperado." You'd say something like "I work in banks" or "I've done some railroad work." It took me a long time just to say, "I'm a writer."*
>
> — RAY BLOUNT JR.

317. Write what you are. Start with "I am..."

318. Write what you tell people when they ask what you do. Write what they respond if you say you're a writer. If they tell you they'd write a book if they had the time, what do you say?

I am in high school. I am thirteen years old and six feet seven inches tall and I weigh 125 pounds. I look like a skeleton. I have grown a foot in the last year. I am the tallest person in the school, taller even than the teachers. Everybody laughs at me.

— MICHAEL CRICHTON

319. Write about how you looked in high school. Too tall, too short, or just fine? Write about your hair and your skin and the shoes you wore.

320. Write about a time someone laughed at you or bullied you in school. Or a time when you were the bully.

I became aware of a growing rift in myself. There was one side, and I identified it as male, that was eager to go into any kind of danger, and loved nothing more than to sit with a group of strangers, speaking a strange language, in the middle of nowhere. And there was another side, which I identified as female, that wanted only to stay at home. I could hear their voices at different times, even at different times of day.

— SUSAN BRIND MORROW

321. Write about your adventurous side, where it wants to go, what it needs to experience. How does this side of you deal with danger? Does this side feel male to you or female? Or both?

322. Write about the part of you that wants to stay home. Why it wants or needs to stay home, what staying home is about.

> *While I fear that we're drawn to what abandons us, and to what seems most likely to abandon us, in the end I believe we're defined by what embraces us.*
>
> — J. R. MOEHRINGER

323. Write about a time when you were abandoned. Or write what or who you fear may abandon you in the future.

324. Write about what embraces you. A partner, a friend, a whole family, a church, a temple, a community, your dog? What does being embraced entail?

If a friend of yours loses someone, write them a letter full of love. You need them, these letters, to help you get through the days and the evenings somehow. You open them, you read, you search for the mot juste, *and you always find it.... Write, write, write. Do not miss one opportunity to do it. If you have the choice between writing and not writing, always choose to write. Not a single letter is out of place.*

— Geneviève Jurgensen

325. Write a letter to a friend, whether or not they've lost someone. Thank him or her for something they've done, or send wishes for a happy birthday, holiday, or anniversary. Or write just to send love.

> *In my experience, whatever happens clings to us like barnacles on the hull of a ship, slowing us slightly, both uglifying and giving us texture. You can scrape all you want, you can, if you have money, hire someone else to scrape, but the barnacles will come back, or at least leave a blemish on the steel.*
>
> — NICK FLYNN

326. Write about your own barnacles. How have the events of your past slowed you? How have they given you texture and depth? Write about one specific barnacle and your attempt to remove it or reconcile with it.

327. Write a list of questions to which you expect no answers.

328. Write a list of questions to which you urgently need answers.

> *The verbs we live — that is, the actions we take — create the landscape of our lives. The verbs we live, the actions we take, the story we frame over those actions...*
>
> — PATTI DIGH

329. Write a list of verbs for your life. Consider the relationship of the verbs/actions to the story of your life.

330. Write a list of verbs that your characters live. Do they strive, resist, linger, attempt, love, hate, or, like real people, live a contradictory mix of actions?

> *The wilderness in which I wandered as a young boy,*
> *believing myself forever lost, never to reach a destina-*
> *tion, I have now come to believe is precisely the place to*
> *be. There is no lasting comfort, it seems to me, in the*
> *safe landing. Better to stay in flight, take the next bus,*
> *relinquish control, trust in happenstance and embrace*
> *impermanence.*
>
> — FRANK LANGELLA

331. Write about a time you were lost. Literally or figuratively.

332. Write about taking the next bus. What's your destination or your character's?

> *But then patience was once the order of the day, and the physical act of writing was close to the operational definition of being a writer at all. Jane Austen wrote at a tiny desk in the parlor, and whenever someone entered the room she would swiftly slip the manuscript under the blotter or in the drawer. Not shy, not threatened, but ever alert to her social duties and somehow thriving on interruption.*
>
> — PAUL MONETTE

333. Write about a time you had to be patient. Or wished you had been. Write about what your body does when you're feeling impatient.

334. Write a scene, true or fictional, in which a person is interrupted while doing something he or she considers to be very important, and is either furious or pretends to be patient with the interruption.

> *I stumbled across a thought in my mind:* Use your life to illuminate something larger. *That's it. That's what we're all called to do.*
>
> — PHYLLIS THEROUX

335. Write about something you've experienced that could illuminate a larger issue. What have you gone through, or what are you living day by day, that might help someone who is going through the same thing?

336. Write your point of view about something in today's news that you can connect with through your own experience.

> *Though everyone is talented and original, often it does not break through for a long time. People are too scared, too self-conscious, too proud, too shy. They have been taught too many things about construction, plot, unity, mass and coherence.*

> — BRENDA UELAND

337. Write about a time you were too self-conscious and scared to accomplish what you hoped to do. What were you scared of? And what are your regrets about not doing it?

338. Write about a specific time that you felt shy. How did your face feel? Your hands? Write a scene in which one of your characters is shy and unable to say what needs to be said.

339. Write about a moment when you realized you were original and talented. What did you do with the realization?

I was inspired by [Amelia] Earhart to do something that at the time felt daring and frightening and possibly very stupid: write a novel. A novel no one had asked for and no one, as far as I knew, was going to read. She inspired me to face the unknown, the empty sky, the blank page.

— JANE MENDELSOHN

340. Write about a time when someone inspired you — to do either something that frightened you or something you hadn't considered. The inspiration can come from a real person or a character from a film or book.

> *Rule of thumb: The more important a call or action is to our soul's evolution, the more Resistance we will feel toward pursuing it.*
>
> — STEVEN PRESSFIELD

341. Write about what's calling to you right now on the deepest level. Write what the voice of resistance is telling you.

342. Write a scene in which a character hears a call to action or change, but resists.

Suspicion is a philosophy of hope. It makes us believe that there is something to know and something worth knowing. It makes us believe there is something rather than nothing. In this sense, sexual jealousy is a form of optimism, if only for philosophers.

— ADAM PHILLIPS

343. Write about something specific that once made you suspicious. Write about whether your suspicions were right. And if so, was it worth finding out about? Did you snoop to find answers?

344. Write about a time you were jealous in a romantic relationship. Write how it felt, what you did, and what you said. Or write about being silent.

> *Emotion resulting from a work of art is only of value when it is not obtained by sentimental blackmail.*
>
> — JEAN COCTEAU

345. Write one dramatic paragraph or page of your story with as much sentimentality as possible. Lard it with as many adverbs and adjectives as you can dream up. Then take everything out that isn't absolutely necessary.

Every one of us — all these Latino men and women, and their children, and the boys in their hip clothes, and the white policemen, and the curious grad students, the ice cream vendor and the happy viejas, *and even Paul and I, two white gay boys with our short hair and outfits out of sync with the neighborhood — we all belong here.*

— MARK DOTY

346. Write about a place that isn't your neighborhood, or maybe not even your country, but where you feel you belong. What is it that makes you feel at home there? What is it about you, if anything, that's out of sync with the place?

The page waits, pretending to be blank. Is that its appeal, its blankness? What else is this smooth and white, this terrifyingly innocent? A snowfall, a glacier? It's a desert, totally arid, without life. But people venture into such places. Why?

— MARGARET ATWOOD

347. Write about the appeal of the blank page for you. Write about the fear of the blank page. What scares you most? What excites you most?

348. Write a love scene that takes place in the snow.

I began to sift through my memory to find the shape of the story. This remembering was a delicate alchemy, part archaeology, part forensics, and — perhaps the most important part — a powerful urge to take that time in my life, those ashes, that sadness and self-destruction, and turn it into something larger and universal. To find the narrative in the tragedy. To make art out of loss.

— DANI SHAPIRO

349. Write about a morning in a particular period of your life when you were heartbroken or depressed. Did you have trouble sleeping, or did you sleep all the time? What did you keep in your refrigerator? What did you eat? What clothes did you wear? As you write the details, look for the shape of a story about this period of your life. Is there a beginning? And then an ending?

350. Write about ashes.

People said: "Oh, be yourself at all costs." But I found that it was not so easy to know just what one's self was. It was far easier to want what other people seemed to want and then imagine that the choice was one's own.

— JOANNA FIELD

351. Write a list of choices you've made in your life.

352. Write about the cost or reward of one of those choices.

353. Write about a time when you felt totally and authentically yourself. Or the opposite.

> *To theorize about how I became a writer, and how writing shapes my life now, requires levels of abstraction and reasoning that are beyond my abilities. But by making brief notes, capturing shards of memory or thought, writing out specific scenes, I began to discover what they meant and how they might cohere.*
>
> — FLOYD SKLOOT

354. Write a list of brief memories from your life. Short sketches of random but specific scenes, remembered words and faces. Don't worry about them connecting or making a lot of sense.

355. Write out one of the scenes from your list. If you're writing nonfiction, maybe memories will surprise you; details might appear that you'd forgotten. If you're writing fiction, try writing memories in your character's voice; trust that your imagination will make up details that will surprise you.

356. Write how your writing can shape your life. How is your life different when you write? How does writing change things?

For surely it is a magical thing for a handful of words, artfully arranged, to stop time. To conjure a place, a person, a situation, in all its specificity and dimensions. To affect us and alter us, as profoundly as real people and things do.

— JHUMPA LAHIRI

357. Write about a house, real or imagined, in all its specificity. Write the smells in the kitchen, the views from the windows, the sheets on the bed, the contents of the hall closet, what's hanging on the walls, how rain pounds on its roof.

358. Write about a person, real or imagined, so specifically that readers will think that they've met this person. Write what this person does for the first thirty minutes of his or her day.

> *It is six a.m., and I am working. I am absentminded,*
> *reckless, heedless of social obligations, etc. It is as it*
> *must be. The tire goes flat, the tooth falls out, there will*
> *be a hundred meals without mustard. The poem gets*
> *written.*
>
> — MARY OLIVER

359. Write down the time and what you are doing right now, this very minute. You're reading this, of course. But why, and are there obligations in your life that you're not dealing with because you're reading and doing writing exercises? Will the poem, the novel, the memoir, the essay get written?

360. Write about a flat tire. It can be one that you've experienced, or you can give it to a character and see how he or she handles it.

361. Write about an ingredient that got forgotten. Did it matter? Or were there consequences?

Repeat after me: "I'm a writer. It's my job. It's what I do."

If you embrace that statement, then you can begin to develop the practice of writing. You go to work every day. You sit your butt in a chair...and you put in your hours just like everyone else who goes to work. But many of us are scared to commit to being a Writer, so we don't commit to the job of writing. Take yourself seriously: Say you're a writer. And if you're a writer, figure out how to do your job.

— ELLEN SUSSMAN

362. Write in your journal, "I'm a writer. It's my job. It's what I do." Know that you are a writer if you're writing. The word *write* is a verb.

363. Write in your journal a plan for how you're going to do your job as a writer. Write down the time each day that you'll sit down to write, even if it's only for fifteen minutes every morning or afternoon. Write it on your calendar too.

> *The days will be warm and I will sit by the sea and write a book about something other than myself, and in the afternoons I will lie in the arms of a longtime lover who will make a truth of permanence.*
>
> — FRANCES LEAR

364. Write a fantasy, a dream, a cherished hope, a goal. What will the weather be like? Where will you be sitting? Will you be alone or with someone? What will you be writing?

Fear, to a great extent, is born of a story we tell our-
selves, and so I chose to tell myself a different story....I
decided I was safe. I was strong. I was brave. Nothing
could vanquish me. Insisting on this story was a form
of mind control, but for the most part, it worked....
Fear begets fear. Power begets power. I willed myself to
beget power. And it wasn't long before I actually wasn't
afraid.

— CHERYL STRAYED

365. Write the story you need to read.

> *We have to continually be jumping off cliffs and developing our wings on the way down.*
>
> — KURT VONNEGUT

Keep going. Let the bits and pieces of exercises help you to write your story, your book, your essay. Sprout wings as you jump off the cliff into optimism.

WHAT THEY WROTE

In class, students inspire one another. Though sometimes they're intimidated and make comparisons ("oh, that's so good/funny/smart," "how can I ever...?" etc.), they also see each other's work grow, and this ultimately gives them courage and inspiration for their own writing. To encourage you, here are responses to prompts in the book, by sixteen of my students. Each is working on a memoir or novel, so many of their exercises circle around the subject of their work in progress. All the exercises were written in five minutes, and (except for slight cutting for clarity and space and a few name changes) they're unedited. The students whose work I've included have taken a number of my classes and have had a lot of practice doing five-minute exercises. Each writer is identified by his or her initials, with full names and a short biography for each student in the section that follows.

An intention about your writing

A pediatrician told me that maybe raising a child is more like creating a space to protect their spirit so that a child can grow into who she is rather than the idea of molding a child. It relates to my journey becoming a writer. I will create a protected space to rest in where I will write, explore, and grow every day, not worrying on that particular day if it is "good" or not, and try to keep the faith that good things will come.

— KK

One thing in your life that stays the same

A daily tide of clients who have sick animals and are short of cash. There's the puppy named Harry with parvovirus, whose owners are shocked — shocked that this puppy they got from a friend for their kids and never took to a vet is dying unless they spend thousands, with no guarantee of survival. And yes, there are waves of singers and actresses who work as masseuses and personal assistants and waiters, whose old pets probably have cancer, something incurable. But these days there are also wives of record producers who've been clients for twenty years and used to give out Mont Blanc pens at three hundred dollars a pop to the entire vet hospital staff at Christmas who are now looking for discounts and cheaper options.

— JAS

Where you live

This is where I live, in a tangle of limbs and boy feet, a pile of stained shirts, large, small, smallest, a stack of dirty plates in the sink stained with agave syrup, and tiny flecks of homemade french-toast skin. Where I live is with the noise of crashing plastic garbage trucks, the demands for hot dogs and pasta Os, the cries for milk or sleep or time without me trying to get something else done, the pleasure of sitting with Vlad after the boys are asleep in their room, Max in the hand-me-down crib with the two bunny blankies and purple plushy anteater, Théo in the mattress on the floor with the toddler railing and the rooster pillow and his red jeep clutched in his hands.

— ME

A time you tried to pay attention

I am sitting across from the neurologist, who is behind his big, brown desk. Piles of papers lie all over it; he makes a temple with his hands, and I notice how his fingers taper and how they almost look polished. He wears a bow tie and parts his hair on the side. He looks really young, younger than I. We are discussing brain surgery, namely the difference between a corpus callosum and a hemispherectomy. We don't know if Sophie is a candidate for surgery yet, but we're discussing the options. I suddenly hover over myself and see my black hair below, my head nodding, mouth talking. The neurologist decides which would be better: snipping the center of the brain to prevent the two sides from communicating or taking one side out completely.

— EA

A time you weren't sure who you were

Mother's Day: I had just had a miscarriage and a follow-up surgery, and I was still tender and sore when Ron and I drove to church that Sunday morning. He had to help me out of the car, and he held my arm as he steered me into the church. We made it to a pew, and I sidestepped down the row. And then the pastor came to the pulpit and asked all the mothers to stand. I looked around. Was I a mother? Just a few weeks ago I had been ten weeks pregnant. Almost all the women were standing. I didn't. I looked around, trying to find more women who remained seated. Had they had miscarriages? Abortions? Had they been trying to get pregnant for years but been unable to conceive? I didn't exactly feel like a mother, but I didn't feel like I wasn't a mother either.

— JR

Your hair

I need my hair blown out, and I can't seem to make that happen. The lady in the salon…a funny kind of word to describe the one-person beauty shop in the one-street town in Montana where I find myself — but that's what the sign says — is too busy to do my hair. She's booked all day today and tomorrow. Where are all these people in this town who are coming to this hair salon? Is there a party happening that I haven't been invited to? I look disconsolate and ask the hairdresser who is cutting and drying a customer on the single chair in the shop if she might want to come in a little early tomorrow morning and blow-dry my hair before her 9:00 AM customer. She looks pained. Torn even. "No," she says, a bit defensively, as if we're already in the middle of a conversation where I've been badgering her to open her door early. "I've made a life decision recently…" I finish her sentence and say, "Oh, that you're going to say no to people." "Yeah," she says, still not bonding with me in the way I had hoped. "Well, I support your decision completely," I say, secretly thinking, if I offer her LA money for the blow-out, will she say yes?

— PB

A ritual in your life

Weekend mornings I open the shades and wake Perry. He always greets me with a smile. I pull the comforter back and the sheets. It's time to get up, I say. I guide his legs to the edge of the bed, direct his feet to the floor. It's easier to get him to stand when his legs are bent, feet to the floor. I hold his hand as we walk gingerly and slowly into the bathroom. I put toothpaste on his toothbrush, guide his hand to his mouth. After a few brushes, I follow up more rigorously, then turn on the faucet to fill his cup with water. He spits out. I put shaving cream on my fingers, spread it on his cheeks, place the razor in his hand. He strokes one side of his face, then the other, then his chin. I finish the spots he missed, rinsing his face of the remaining lather. The morning ritual is done.

— CL

Your mother's kitchen

I hear my mother moving through the kitchen in a tizzy as though the clock is ticking like a time bomb and the baby will explode from my abdomen right before our eyes. My mother hates that kitchen. With its one small window above the sink and its darkly varnished cupboards, it craves sunshine and openness the way she craves nicotine. The kitchen door opens in the same spot where the basement door swings into the room from the stairway below. Both doors have sets of hooks, double and triple hung with coats, and it seems as if there's a crowd of people standing in the doorway jostling one another for position. It's claustrophobic, and the wood used to make the cupboards is cheap — redwood, my mother says, when it should have been oak. Each time a drawer is slid in or out, it shaves sawdust onto the shelf of the cabinet below. On a bad day, my mother can be prone to banging and slamming, and I worry this might be the day when she reduces the kitchen to a pile of splinters. It wouldn't be like the day she set the curtains on fire. That was an accident. Nothing burns like polyester, but my mother's reflexes were good. She saved the pork that had caught fire, and kept the house from burning down. The singed remains of the curtains were thrown in the trash that day, and the lower half of the window stayed bare after that. That's the way things are at our house. If something breaks or goes up in flames, we just make do with what's left. Maybe we'll survive this too.

— DEC

A time you tried to help someone

My parents have been trying to break up for a year. They are still in love. Where is the twenty-five-year-old? I said to my mother last night. There is no twenty-five-year-old — at least give him that! She agreed. We made progress during our talk, me holding her lasagna pan I had washed after dinner and her with her hand on the doorknob of the front door. I think about him every morning when I wake up, she says. She starts to cry again. She says he is obsessed with his book tour, his new iPhone, the new wood floors of the house in Brentwood he moved into last summer, trains for Théo, the perfect martini. My mother tells me he said to her she is like a child, all she wants is passion. You are an adult, I tell her, you know how to love calmly. My father reminds me of my kids — their giddiness, their playfulness, how they compete with one another — Théo throwing things on the floor like a baby, Max trying to climb up chairs and open windows. You need to go talk to someone with him, I tell her. What do you mean? she says. Have you said this to him? Not yet, I say, but I will.

— ME

A time you tried to mend fences

I looked snazzy in my blue blazer and orange tie. I felt smooth with a half pint of Jack Daniel's in my stomach. I was shaking hands and slapping backs of former employers and vet-association officials I had quarreled openly and nastily with. I had fences to mend, and a book to sell, goddamn it, and this was the first step on the yellow brick road. The guy to my left announced the guy to my right, who happened to be a newly transferred senior authority over me in the company I was happily working for. He was also the guy who had taken me under his wing in New York and launched my career in LA: and then raped my girlfriend there after I had moved.

— JAS

Someone you miss

I miss my boys, and I feel like they are not mine anymore. They are offered up to the world now. I don't have them every day, I'm not preparing Eggo waffles or wrapping tacos in foil for their lunch and worrying about whether they will get picked up from car pool. We're not going to Bud's Ice Cream after school, where Zack will get cookies and cream and Paul's tongue will turn blue from bubblegum ice cream. I don't know what kind of ice cream they eat now or what they had for dinner last night or what they had for lunch. Are they hungry?

— CL

A pair of old shoes you own

I bought the boots in Wisconsin. 1979. Winter. I was Christmas shopping for my husband. Hauling the presents in a suitcase somewhere. Wherever it was we spent

Christmas that year. Iowa? Nebraska? His family or mine. Both of those places probably. I bought him a chessboard made by a local artisan. Dark wood. Light wood. I don't know what kind. The pieces came in a wooden box. I can't remember if he ever used the set. But the boots. There they were in the window.

I had them resoled last year, and the guy at the shoe repair looked at them and whistled. "Don't ever get rid of these," he said. "The workmanship no longer exists." So many things no longer exist.

— DEC

A pair of shoes your character owns

Rosita Hernandez is gone now, but her shoes are not. They are neatly lined against the wall next to the folded-up wheelchair in what was her bedroom at the hacienda. She has been gone six months, but her grandson, Jimmy, still keeps her black leather shoes, her lace dresses, and her Bible just where she left them. Rosita Hernandez thinks he is afraid that if he moves them, she will come back during the night and rescue them from the trunk, or the burning fire, or the package he has made for the poor Indians at the Taos pueblo.

Maybe he is afraid that she will walk back into his life, and she will.

— LS

How your family shaped you

I was shaped by my mother. The voices in my head are her.... Voices of fear. Voices of pain. They will live in me, long after she is gone. The first five years of doing spays and neuters, I heard these voices. "What are you doing? Be careful. Tie that vessel off!!" My mother knows nothing about doing surgery on a dog, but her voice is there, telling me to check this, don't forget that, you stupid bastard. I would sweat hard during surgery those first five years, until I figured out how to make the voices wait outside the surgery room, with all the other contaminated stuff.

The look of fear in a dog's eyes before we put an IV in for surgery is the same look of fear I've seen in my mom: before her own surgery, before guests came over for dinner, when my dad came home late from work. That fear lives inside me, and also two houses down, waving at me as I go on my way to work.

— JAS

Why you can't write when you want to write

You can't write because they are still living. What would they say?

You can't write because you are known and it will follow you.

Writing can stalk you.

It traps you into a location that you may have to defend.

Sometimes you don't have the permission to write it — from yourself.

You don't write because it may not be deep enough to finger the truth.

You cannot always get to what you want.

The space seems to be larger than the activity, so I wait until I get the space.

It's too serious.

— TMH

What you smelled when you opened an old trunk or attic door

After my father had died, we were searching out the far recesses of the house before it was to be sold. Grief still hung in the air, and I was visiting from Los Angeles, where I'd recently moved.

I venture to the attic, pull the string, allow the trap-door to open with the folded-up stairs, unfold them. Climb up and pull the string on the lightbulb. The smell of cedar. That familiar smell. This is where, as a kid, I'd wandered and nearly fell through the fiberglass batting that lay on the floor. Far in the corner, past the light, there were some battered boxes. These my father had hidden once when my mother had been on one of her "Throw out the past!" rants. I grab them and bring them downstairs to the den, searching for clues.

— RR

A memory about money

I remember the times that my parents fought over money. There was never enough money in our house. Money. Adding machine, cigarette smoke, and swearing at the kitchen table after I'd gone to bed. I never had enough money either. In my high school I worked as the janitor, sweeping floors after my friends had gone home. In college I dusted library books, scraped plates, sold blood, modeled nude.

My husband and I fought about money, too. He spent the last couple of bucks at McDonald's on a burger instead of filling out the job application. We lived on Bisquick then. A decade later money piled up. In 1981 we had a secret handshake — three fingers, four fingers and a knuckle bump that signified his first big fat law firm salary. Eventually the money buried us.

— DEC

Feeling crazy and unhinged

"Go back to sleep," I hiss at Perry. It's the middle of the night, and we are in Mammoth, in the only room that is habitable in the condo we just bought. Two twin beds line the walls of the room, and disoriented, he keeps waking up and trying to climb into my bed. It must be strange for him, being in a new room, us in separate beds. But at 3:00 AM I am tired, and I just want to sleep. I push him back onto his bed. "This is your bed," I say as I cover him again with quilts, climb back to my bed. I stare at the wooden beams, visible in the moonlight from the window. How long can I continue doing this? Will the day come when I have to put him in a home? I want this to be over. I want to get him to sleep. In the middle of the night, I'm no longer the kind caregiver I am during the day. "Go to sleep," I hiss again as he starts to get up. I move to his bed, see the confusion in his face when I turn on the light. I try a different tack. "These are single beds. There is no room for the two of us. You have to sleep in this bed. When we go home, we will have our bigger bed." His eyes soften in comprehension. He sinks into sleep.

— CL

Something you discovered about your grandmother's life

My nana Frances was a small, striking woman. I spent nearly every Saturday with her when I was in the seventh grade. My mother would drop me off at her apartment and then speed away. Nana Frances peppered her conversations with sentences like "I wish I was dead," "What the hell difference does it make?" and when she'd come visit us, she'd say just before we drove her home, "I'm going to go home and stick my head in the oven."

When she was in high school, the Boston Conservatory of Music offered her a full scholarship because she was a wonderful pianist. She wasn't "allowed" to take it because her family was poor, and she was expected to go to work as soon as she graduated the twelfth grade. I didn't know this, of course, back when we'd circle the baseball field in Cleveland Circle and I'd implore, "Live for me, Nana! Live for me!" It wasn't until years later, long after Nana had died at the age of ninety-seven of natural causes, that my mother told me this.

— RR

A time you did something unlike yourself

I circled the cologne aisle at the Williamsburg Pharmacy, keeping my head down while watching the man at the soda counter off to my left and the old lady behind the cosmetics counter to my right. I lingered at the toys just across, knowing this would deflect suspicion, but it wasn't a new Matchbox car or softball I wanted. This weekend there was a school dance, and it was Hai Karate, the cologne of choice for seventh-grade boys, I wanted. I turned around to find old Miss Kate trying on lipstick and the soda man filling a milk-shake cup. I slipped the bottle in my coat pocket.

— RD

A time you procrastinated

We had held each other for weeks or had it been months? Time now had its own terms. Life had its new rules and we could only…That was it really, we could only do what was in front of us now. For the past two years we had loved and laughed, cried and lived our day-to-day in the happiness of us. For the past two months we had not made love. It wasn't a plan it — just was not. Too many pains, the need for more drugs, the time to sleep, the knowing tomorrow would be better. Desire had been hung in the closet along with our good clothes. Desire would come out when we could do our night on the town. She reached for me that night. It was an unexpected, unspoken request, and perhaps she knew. It would be the last time, but I put it aside for another time. There was no time again. I have wondered about what was lost and if she knew I wanted but didn't.

— TMH

A time you drove away

Up. I needed to go up North. To drive and keep on driving. If I reached Canada, good. If I ended up in a smashed heap on the side of the road, better. I wanted out. I didn't deserve to live — didn't deserve the love of my children and husband. I was an adulterer. A married woman in love with another woman. And there was no escape.... But to drive.

Speeding on PCH, the surfers and happy summer beachgoers a blur. I had to get out and Up. I hoped to find a cabin in the woods. A place where I could curl up in a window seat with cranberry and forest-green pillows surrounding me. I'd write the story of my life there. Write something so when I was gone, people would know I wasn't so bad.

I planned to keep driving till I left California and found myself well into Oregon. Maybe the Cascades. I pulled over in a place north of Malibu where huge boulders divide and the road breaks through them. In between these two rocks — in between these two hard places, I called my husband. "Mark," I sobbed. "I have something to tell you."

— BL

A character driving away

Even in the dark Eloise could make out the spreading pool of blood from the man's head. Drive, she thought, just drive. He had darted out from the median just underneath the 405 Freeway overpass on Wilshire, across three lanes of traffic. She hadn't actually seen the car in front of her make contact but she had heard the sound — a thud, a screech — and she had seen the man just moments before, a dark shadow teetering on a curb, then a flash of cloth speeding across, a blur of metal, and the children, the children sat in the back.

— EJ

A time you didn't know what was going on

When Nina gets upset, her Icelandic accent comes out. Not her Austrian German, which she spoke only to her mother for seven years, and then for the next ten in Vienna, but her native Icelandic, which she navigated the world with, for her first seven years alive.

"I didn't SEENK I was doing anything wrong," she

says, through tears, in a discussion where she says she will take her cat and a few things, and leave me.

"What?? Sink? What sink?" I say.

"SEENK!"

"See what?"

"I didn't...oh..." She starts to sob.

"Oh, think," I say.

Suddenly I realize that this Battle-Ax, this harridan, this llama, this alien intruder, is the partner I've chosen to navigate my life with, this person who at age thirteen protested the Vietnam War, the Franco regime murdering its civilians, the human rights abuses in Uganda, the bashings of gays in Berlin, and the beatings of Palestinians in Jerusalem, who herself was beaten on the head by Viennese police, kicked out by her mother, abused by her stepfather, and betrayed by teachers and employers.

"Don't go," I say.

— JAS

A time your mother...

I remember the time that my mother was annoyed with me for making such a mess around the apartment, so when my father and sister went out, she had me put away all my clothes that I had flung in various corners of our two-bedroom apartment in Queens and dishes that I had left in my room and schoolbooks that I had strewn about the living room. We divided the living room from the dining alcove with an iron railing about three feet high and four feet long. Along with our French provincial furniture, it was an attempt at elegance, to have a dining area separate from the kitchen and not quite in the living room. So I worked for what I remember to be hours but was more likely just a single hour — the apartment was not so large as to have been able to create a daylong mess — and then my father and sister came home. She took off her sweater and jacket and tossed them both over the railing that I just cleaned off of blouses and pants that never made it to my closet. I was furious. I turned to her and screamed, "Take — off — your — clothes!" She looked at me in horror and began to unbutton her blouse.

— PB

Trying to do the right thing

The girl in me was gone. I woke up the morning after my mother died and asked not what was I going to wear today but what does she wear to be buried in? Does she need a bra? Pierced earrings or clip-on? Sling backs or ballet flats? Does the funeral home choose the lipstick, or do I bring one from her makeup bag? Can there be a wrong way to do this? A right way? Does success or failure enter the conversation when you bury people?

— FSD

A setting for your fiction

It's always gray inside, perpetually gray. And littered. Losing tickets scatter the floor, always an extra heap just outside the tall, wide, blue garbage pails. So many distracted losers unable even to get their debris hooked into the pail. It can be sunny outside or in the clubhouse, warm even, but inside general admission at the track, gray, always gray; rancid smell of sweat and cigar smoke, cigarettes and urine. Always urine, swirling in perceptible plumes of distilled vapors.

— EJ

Remembering the time...

I remember the time my sister sent me the wallet she'd made for me. I was eight. It was blue with red "gimp" attaching the sides together. She was twelve years older than me and lived in St. Louis, and I knew she was in a special hospital. I don't know now how I knew it, but I did. This wallet with a silver snap. And a fold-over pocket. I kept it for years. Too guilty to not keep it. This is what they did there? Arts and crafts? I picture the room where she'd made it the moment it lands at first in my hands. Sunny and big. Light pouring in over long cafeteria tables. People with problems, making wallets.

— RR

A gift you didn't want

My husband traded in my original iPhone for the newest version without asking me. "Merry Christmas!" he said.

I burst into tears. My years of text messages with my best friend were gone. She had died a few months before, and all I had left of her voice were in those daily texts, which I looked at over and over again.

"I'm buying the red shoes."

"I'm watching my baby go off to high school this morning."

"Help, we're in the emergency ward!"

"How r u?"

"Luv u sis!"

"Test results bad. Call me."

She was really gone.

— JOF

A funeral you attended

What kind of a god allows a child to lose his parents? A knowing god? An evil god? It was a good question. One that I asked myself more than a few times since last Thursday. But here I was in a church full of suits and panty hose and high heels and black black black, who all knew who I was, but I didn't know them. I'd gone from being Michael's daughter to one who god had handpicked to give an abundance of material to, for a strange priest's sermon. Is this what it's like to be a celebrity? I wondered. All eyes on you, staring with recognition.

— FSD

Your barnacles

I was born with it and I will die with it — but it took me half my lifetime to learn to live with it and eventually to love it. My Asian Face. Once my "oriental" face. Now my proudly Japanese American face, one that matches my two daughters adopted from China, also born with and living with their Asian faces — their now American faces. As a child, I wanted to look like Malibu Barbie or Skipper, her cute cousin, or the blonde Breck shampoo girls with blue eyes and long eyelashes, whose golden locks glistened in the sunlight. Instead, I had dark eyes the neighborhood kids called "slanty" and a "squished" nose that wouldn't hold up the sunglasses that would hide those eyes and help me blend in.

— JOF

Losing your virginity

I hate this story. I don't know how to tell it and still sound normal. The bare facts: I was twenty-eight and a half. Too old, but I had wanted to wait until marriage. I didn't exactly make it to the wedding night — we slept together on New Year's Eve the year we got engaged — so I was able to hold off until I met the man I married. That is, if you don't count blow jobs as sex.

— JR

A favorite meal

We ate shrimp and grits at a small round table, and we drank a lot of wine. We drank so much wine that I drew stick figures on a napkin proving that I wasn't a prude, and you leaned so far back in your chair (you might have been laughing) that it tipped over. We might have been screaming with laughter, as far as I know, the rest of the people in the restaurant receding, their mouths open, silent. Years later, I picked you up from a Greyhound bus station in Nashville, Tennessee, trailing an enormous suitcase. You fixed my air conditioner and swept out my apartment, and when I came home from my shift, I lay on the bed and you on a sleeping bag beside me and we talked in the darkness, and we talked through the years on the phone and in letters and now over polenta and eggs, and no one makes me laugh harder.

— EA

A family photograph

The child played among her grandmother's things in the great bedroom. Pictures of her mother as a child looked down on her from the mahogany dresser. She loved the lace cloth that dressed every surface, and it was with a gentleness, as if she knew she were probing beyond the allowable, that she opened the trunk under the window. As she lifted the heavy top, voices from the dining room got louder, words became perceptible. *He's a good man*, her grandmother said. *You know nothing* were her mother's words. The little girl found the plastic bag she was looking for, unzipped, and pulled the folds of white fabric, slippery and shiny, threads of white gold, a princess dress, from its satchel. *I'm leaving him*, her mother's voice.

— EJ

A time you felt the call to do something but ignored it

Ideas, thoughts come to me when I'm driving in my car, on the 10 Freeway east towards work. My mind is fresh, alive in the morning, and I come up with brilliant phrases, narratives I want to develop. Sometimes I fumble in my purse for an index card and a pen to write a cryptic note that I can never read again or remember what the thought was.

Ideas, thoughts come to me when I sit in one meeting after another, listen to another person drone on about the cycle of continuous improvement, view another Power-Point presentation with a circle but different words, and I want to bolt from the room and close the door to my office and tell the secretary to not transfer any calls so I could jot or write my notes for the next chapter or the connective tissue between chapters or a vignette I just remembered.

But I sit patiently through one round of meetings, then the next, answer emails, endure the round of questions from staff, grab a quick lunch to eat at my desk, and by the time I look up it's 6:00 and time to start the commute home.

— CL

A time you cried uncontrollably

Alone, at my college graduation, dumped by my girlfriend. Rejected at first try to vet school. Jobless. Future-less. Nowhere to go, except back to my parents' home.

The plane ride was two thousand miles. I wore a blue blazer, light blue Oxford shirt, tan chinos, and brown loafers. Because I knew that would please my mother. But in fact I was way overdressed for the job I would be doing, loading off-price clothes onto trucks in Union City, CA, to be driven to Ross Dress for Less stores across the country. I'd be working alongside guys who wore wife-beater T-shirts and had large tattoos that said "WHITE" all the way down one arm and "pride" all the way down the other.

The man sitting next to me on the plane, also wearing a blue Oxford shirt, with a red-checkered tie and a black suit, smiled at me and said, "Hello." We'd be sitting next to each other for another five and a half hours.

"How are you?" said the man.

I burst into tears and started sobbing. It was hard to breathe. I cried for the whole five and a half hours.

— JAS

A time you were dressed inappropriately

I thought we were appropriate. Myself in my flowing pastel skirt, sandals, and loose white shirt (white being the purest and most spiritual of all colors), my son in his summer plaid collared button-down shirt and gray jeans, and my daughter in a tight light-blue dress. The eve of the Day of Atonement. Our first time back into temple in, well, ever. I took my children to temple that year in an effort to reach back into our Jewish roots and find some grounding. We had reserved family seats in the big sanctuary, no less. When we entered, I knew something was amiss. Everyone was wearing black suits. Everyone. Funereal. We were the only ones in pastels. People were staring at the Jewish Frauds in their presence.

— BL

Your character's parents

It was good to hold the slender book of sonnets in her hand, pressed to her chest, after the funeral. She watched her mother flit among old friends, her father's cronies, business partners, reacquainting herself to them after years of absence, her long mink coat, it was cold grave-side but still, Eloise felt the fur, the diamonds were her mother's prize, her way of saying look at me, I've won, I've outlived the bastard. And poor Annalisa, the widow, still too young to even know what she lost (Eloise hears the murmurs, what was he thinking? Did xxx go in the sack?). But the sonnets, the inscription to her mother in a light scrawl that is proof to her father's youth and innocence and great love, what delicate curves to his handwriting, for Eloise this was the truth. Her father loved her mother, of this Eloise has no doubt.

— EJ

A nontraditional wedding

We wanted to break free of the rituals my sisters and brother dutifully followed in their wedding, the escorting of the bride down the aisle, the special knife to cut the wedding cake, the showers for the bride, the little wedding favors. We were more progressive, innovative. Our wedding was at the Brazilian Room in Tilden Park in Berkeley. No sit-down dinner, we found Trumpetvine Catering, our chocolate buttercream cake from the Buttercup Bakery. No line of bridesmaids and ushers, just us, a best man, and maid of honor. I didn't need my brother to walk me down the aisle, I was an independent woman. But on the day of the wedding, I saw the hurt in my brother's eyes, saw how frazzled Perry was when they asked him where the chairs should go, where the flowers should be. I gave myself in to my mother and sisters, who kept me sequestered in a room because it was bad luck for the groom to see the bride. I let my mother festoon me with jade and gold necklaces like they do in China. I was secretly grateful that my sisters tied together Jordan almonds with pink netting and printed ribbons that said Perry and Cynthia, August 15, 1982.

— CL

One thing you can't control

My son says no to Disneyland. It is his sister's eleventh birthday, and we have woken up on this Thursday and broken the joyous news that instead of going to school, she is going to Disneyland. Our son by luck doesn't have school today. It is my hope that we can pull this together and celebrate Phoebe, the four of us.

I tell him at 7:30, we are going to Disneyland. He stirs, says, "I'm too tired," and rolls over back to sleep. I can smell the adolescent boy smell in his room. It pervades the air.

"Are you sure? Don't you want to come celebrate?"

"Too tired," he mumbles.

I close the door.

We get in the car and drive. Part of me is relieved. This is her day. I worry that if Sawyer comes, his autistic needs will drive the day as they often do. We will always be doing that dance of accommodating him even when we don't know we are doing that. This day we get in the car and go. I can focus. We can focus on her, and yet the victory is hollow. Underneath, I have left part of myself at home.

— KK

A time it became clear what you wanted to do

I hate my job. I don't want to work another weekend. Four years of college, three years of law school. I landed the prime job in a top LA law firm. This should be my dream come true, but it's not. As I transition from the 10 eastbound to the 110 north, I can't bear to exit at 3rd Street and disappear into the office building for hours, billable hours, and more billable hours.

Exit, I tell myself. Exit and get to work. I can't. I can't. What about the deadline? I've got to write a draft of that brief. I'll just go for a little drive; then I'll come back and work late. Just a little drive. I keep going. North on the 110 and then over to the 101 north. I drive and I drive — the bright blue Pacific appears to the west — Ventura. Then on to Santa Barbara, my college home. My paradise. The calm comes with each mile traveled. I pull over to my favorite secret spot and sit on the rocks. I close my eyes. The sun warms my face. I begin to write novels in my mind, not briefs.

— JOF

Fighting over something trivial to avoid the real problem

Bills. He is obsessed with them. Unlike me, he opens them right away. Inevitably, he freaks. "Why is there a ninety-dollar charge from FedEx Kinko's?"

I sigh. I've tried various strategies to temper his freak-outs, but they don't seem to be working. "Remember I told you I was FedEx-ing the Christmas gifts to your family? Remember I told you not to freak out when you see the ninety-dollar charge from FedEx Kinko's?" He wracks his brain. I think he remembers, but there is a whole list of items on the bill, and we'll go through them one by one. The only time I've seen him not spaz out over a bill was once when he opened it and reviewed it and I stood waiting, tense, and he was like, "Okay."

"How much?" I asked.

"Eleven dollars."

"Eleven dollars?"

So eleven dollars is the credit card bill I need to aim

for if I want to avoid a money fight? One night he was stressing about our expenses again. I said, "I make more than most of my girlfriends." I said, "At least I make some money writing — not a lot, but it's not horrible."

"Well, they contribute," he said.

Ah. So that was the real issue. They had given their husbands children.

— JR

A time you tried to control something

Friday night. Shabbat candles in the kitchen. I'm eleven. It doesn't matter what has preceded this moment at dusk. It's G-d's time now. I stand by my mother in front of the kitchen window. I hate her today. "Wait!" I demand. "Wait! Before you light them!"

The window has to be open an inch. I have decided this. Decided that G-d must come in through this space — this breeze. She opens the window. It's too open now. I'm upside down inside. Churning.

"That's too much!" I say.

I won't let her light them. I close it more. Then open it another fraction. Maybe, maybe if I just let it land exactly right, this will all be better. I will feel peace.

— RR

A time you took a chance

Of course I had a plan. I wish I could remember more, but it slips through almost a steady faucet of loss. I can see the scene at dinner. We had the restaurant to ourselves. I remember the table, the room, the hope about the future. I remember butterflies when we were served dessert, the time was coming close. My hands began to sweat as new topics were invented to discuss. Was the time now? Was it foolish? Would I look foolish? I remember I slid out of my chair and onto my knee. I remember her smile. I remember when time started. It started that night.

— TMH

A time you didn't run

I wasn't looking for trouble. But there he was. Billy was helping run the audition for a theater company I wanted into. I knew that feeling. The electricity running through the center of my body. I ignored it, discouraged it, pulled the plug a hundred times in my mind. Billy was married to the director. I was engaged. I kept my distance. He kept his. Still, we knew. I drove over one of those concrete parking lot things after rehearsal one night. It pulled off my muffler. "I'll drive you home," Billy said. The two of us in his Volkswagen. My dark street. "I'm going to kiss you," he said after he'd pulled to the curb. I could have flung open the car door and run. I didn't.

— DEC

A time you couldn't see

The contact lens was gone in the blink of my right eye, the one corrected for distance. I put my hot dinner from

Whole Foods on the seat next to me and looked up to see only black and gray shapes out the windshield. I turned slowly and looked in the lighted mirror. It might be stuck to an eyelash, common for this new pair, the kind you could sleep in. I reached for my spare glasses but they were gone, being outfitted with updated, ever thicker lenses. Could I drive once I got out under the street-lights? What choice did I have? I was ten miles from home, I knew no one here. My reading left eye would have to guide me. I stared down the boulevard, squeezing my right eye closed. No cars, no pedestrians. I pulled out onto the road where another intersection soon faced me. Few streetlights here, was that someone in the crosswalk?

— RD

Something that made your character suspicious

Senora Rosita suspected that her grandson, Jimmy, was not in his right mind. He had a birthmark underneath his left eye, which she told him was the mark of God on his face, but now she was beginning to believe that it might be the mark of the Devil. He was spending too much time with his drama teacher, Senor Cordova, who everyone knew liked boys and men better than women. Certainly, men in Trampas sometimes visited the barns to rid them-selves of urges when their wives would not oblige, but a physical relationship between two men was insupport-able. She tolerated that Jimmy stayed in his room for hours drawing women in fancy clothes which he copied from back issues of Vogue, or pictures of Christ on the cross, his face bloody and tear stained. But now he was spending all his time at school rehearsing the Christmas play with Senor Cordova, ignoring his artwork and leaving her alone in her bed waiting for him to change her soiled sheets.

— LS

Your best friend in high school

Amy Garbstein, with her hot piglike face, is staring me down in the lunchroom again. She's appeared out of nowhere to interrupt my daydream. Her eyes slowly give me the once-over.

"Is your hair wet?" she demands.

"What? No…"

I answer too slowly for her, and she smirks then brushes past me. I know she's tried to insult me, but I can't for the life of me figure out why. Or even how.

Oh, she must mean my hair looks dirty. I know it isn't.

My best friend, Judy, upon hearing this story, decides she'll settle my score. I'm entirely too shy to do so. I watch her march up to Amy, take in every inch of her from top to bottom, then oink like a pig before moving on.

— RR

Your name — who named you this and why

Have you ever met a Phyllis that was twenty-five, five feet eight inches tall, and weighed 120 pounds? Let me answer that for you — you have not! Picture the Phyllises you know from TV — Cloris Leachman on the *Rhoda* show, the matronly, passive Phyllis on *The Office* — Phyllises are always overweight or loud mouthed or past middle age. That is why at various stages of my life, I renamed myself Angelica or Susan Rainbow or, in an attempt to embrace my first name but temper the stereotypes, I changed my last name and became Phyllis Springday. I defy anyone to find a Phyllis who was born after 1959. It's like there was some sort of decree that ended the Phyllis scourge, never to return as trendy or retro-cool like Rose or Sophie. I remember the day my mother told me that she really was looking for a name that began with an *F*, but all she could think of was Frances and she didn't like the one Frances she knew, so she got creative and chose an *F*-sounding name, Phyllis. What was she thinking? I could have been Farrah.

— PB

STUDENT CONTRIBUTORS

ELIZABETH AQUINO has been published in several literary journals, magazines, and online, as well as in the *Los Angeles Times* and *Spirituality and Health*. She blogs daily at www.elizabethaquino.blogspot.com.

PHYLLIS BERGER has published personal essays in the *Huffington Post* and is currently writing travel pieces for the Peter Greenberg Worldwide website, PeterGreenberg.com.

DENISE EMANUEL CLEMEN has written essays and short stories that have been published in *Rattling Wall*, *Literary Mama*, *Two Hawks Quarterly*, and the *Georgetown Review*, and she has received an honorable mention for the Georgetown Review Prize. She blogs at http://leavingdivorceville.blogspot.com.

ROB DALY produces and films book trailers for authors. His own work has been published in *Westways Magazine* and at neworldreview.com. He blogs at www.RobertDaly.org.

MAGDALENA EDWARDS was born in Santiago, Chile, and has a PhD in comparative literature. She has published and edited numerous articles and essays, and is working on a memoir.

JERI OKAMOTO FLOYD has published essays, articles, and columns in *Guideposts*, *Families with Children from China*, the *Loyola of Los Angeles Law Review*, and the Nikkei Chronicles series. Her memoir in progress is about growing up with an Asian American face.

THOMAS MERCER HARTMAN is a designer and artist who tells stories through multimedia and environmental works. He is now writing a memoir of lessons about dying learned through the loss of his wife.

ERICA JAMIESON is the author of essays and short fiction that have appeared in *Self Magazine*, *Lilith Magazine*, *Switchback*, and the anthology *About My Mother*. She is currently at work on a novel.

KATHLEEN KATIMS is working on a memoir about raising a child with autism.

CYNTHIA LIM lives in Los Angeles with her husband and is working on a memoir about his brain injury. Her essays have appeared in the *Legendary*, *Hawai'i Pacific Review*, *Rougarou*, and *RiverSedge*.

BARBARA LODGE has written essays that have appeared in the anthologies *Exit Laughing* and (under her pen name, Leigh Stuart) *Dear John, I Love Jane*. Other essays of hers have been published in the *Los Angeles Times*, the *Sun* magazine, and *Whole Life Times*. She is currently at work on a memoir.

JENNY ROUGH has written for numerous magazines, newspapers, ezines, and anthologies. Visit her website at jennyrough.com.

RUTH RUDNICK, an alumnus of the Second City theater in Chicago, has appeared on numerous TV shows, including *Curb Your Enthusiasm* and *NCIS*. She is now writing a childhood memoir.

JAMES A. SHORE is the pen name of a practicing veterinarian in Los Angeles. He has published essays and is at work on a memoir.

FRANCESCA SMITHWICK-DRIVER has had an essay published in the *Los Angeles Times* and is currently writing a memoir about being the last surviving member of her family.

LOREN STEPHENS has published essays and short stories in numerous publications, including the *Jewish Women's Literary Annual*, the *North Atlantic Review*, the *Los Angeles*

Times, and the *Chicago Tribune*. She is president of Write Wisdom and currently at work on a novel based on her Japanese husband's family history.

ACKNOWLEDGMENTS

Contrary to popular thought, writing a book is not always a solitary endeavor. Sometimes it gets written with a crowd. With gratitude, many thanks, and much love to my crowd: the sixteen students who showed up at my house to write five-minute exercises; my agent, Lisa Erbach Vance, and everybody at the Aaron M. Priest Literary Agency, especially Arleen and Aaron; my editor, Jason Gardner, copilot for four of my books, plus everybody at New World Library, especially Monique Muhlenkamp, Kristen Cashman, Tracy Cunningham, Munro Magruder, Tona Pearce Myers, and Mark Colucci; Linda Venis and the staff at the Writers' Program at UCLA Extension; the writers I've quoted in this book; my family — immediate members and extended; and always and forever, my husband, R., who has the heart and patience of a saint.

BIBLIOGRAPHY

Ackerman, Diane. *A Natural History of the Senses*. New York: Vintage Books, 1991.

———. *A Slender Thread: Rediscovering Hope at the Heart of Crisis*. New York: Random House, 1997.

Allison, Dorothy. *Two or Three Things I Know for Sure*. New York: Plume, 1996.

Angelou, Maya. *Even the Stars Look Lonesome*. New York: Random House, 1997.

Atchity, Kenneth. *A Writer's Time: A Guide to the Creative Process from Vision through Revision*. New York: Norton, 1986.

Atwood, Margaret. *Murder in the Dark: Short Fictions and Prose Poems*. London: Virago Press, 1994.

Bass, Rick. *Why I Came West*. Boston: Houghton Mifflin, 2008.

Bateson, Mary Catherine. *Composing a Life*. New York: Plume, 1990.

Bayley, John. *Elegy for Iris*. New York: Picador, 2000.

Bender, Sue. *Plain and Simple: A Woman's Journey to the Amish*. San Francisco: HarperSanFrancisco, 1991.

Benedict, Elizabeth, ed. *Mentors, Muses & Monsters: 30 Writers on the People Who Changed Their Lives*. New York: Free Press, 2009.

Bettelheim, Bruno. *The Uses of Enchantment: The Meaning and Importance of Fairy Tales*. New York: Vintage Books, 1977.

Bland, Jared, ed. *Finding the Words: Writers on Inspiration,*

Desire, War, Celebrity, Exile, and Breaking the Rules. Toronto: Emblem, 2011.

Bode, Richard. *Beachcombing at Miramar: The Quest for an Authentic Life*. New York: Warner Books, 1996.

Bracken, Peg. *The I Hate to Cook Book: More Than 180 Quick and Easy Recipes*. New York: Harcourt, Brace, 1960.

Brodie, Deborah, ed. *Writing Changes Everything: The 627 Best Things Anyone Ever Said about Writing*. New York: St. Martin's Press, 1997.

Broyard, Anatole. *Intoxicated by My Illness: And Other Writings on Life and Death*. Compiled and edited by Alexandra Broyard. New York: Clarkson Potter, 1992.

Canin, Ethan. "How Did Your Life Turn Out?" Interview by Jane Rosenzweig. *Atlantic Online*, November 25, 1998. www.theatlantic.com/past/docs/unbound/bookauth /ba981125.htm.

Carver, Raymond. "Gravy." In *A New Path to the Waterfall: Poems*. New York: Atlantic Monthly Press, 1989.

Chambers, Veronica. "Hair." In Fiffer and Fiffer, *Body*.

Coles, Robert. *The Call of Stories: Teaching and the Moral Imagination*. Boston: Houghton Mifflin, 1989.

Colette. *Break of Day*. Translated by Enid McLeod. New York: Farrar, Straus and Cudahy, 1961.

Cooper, Bernard. *Maps to Anywhere*. Athens: University of Georgia Press, 1990.

Crichton, Michael. *Travels*. New York: Knopf, 1988.

Cunningham, Michael. *The Hours*. New York: Farrar, Straus and Giroux, 1998.

Datcher, Michael. *Raising Fences: A Black Man's Love Story*. New York: Riverhead Books, 2002.

Daum, Meghan. *Life Would Be Perfect If I Lived in That House*. New York: Vintage Books, 2011.

de Botton, Alain. "On Writing." In Bland, *Finding the Words*.

Dederer, Claire. *Poser: My Life in Twenty-Three Yoga Poses*. New York: Farrar, Straus and Giroux, 2011.

DeSalvo, Louise. *On Moving: A Writer's Meditation on New Houses, Old Haunts, and Finding Home Again*. New York: Bloomsbury, 2009.

Dillard, Annie. *Pilgrim at Tinker Creek*. New York: Harper's Magazine Press, 1974.

————. *The Writing Life*. New York: Harper & Row, 1989.

Doty, Mark. *Firebird: A Memoir*. New York: Harper Perennial, 2000.

————. *Still Life with Oysters and Lemon*. Boston: Beacon Press, 2002.

Dunn, Samantha. *Faith in Carlos Gomez: A Memoir of Salsa, Sex, and Salvation*. New York: Owl Books, 2005.

Dunn, Stephen. "The Unsaid." In *Good Poems for Hard Times*, edited by Garrison Keillor. New York: Viking, 2005.

Dunne, Peter. *Emotional Structure: Creating the Story beneath the Plot; A Guide for Screenwriters*. Fresno, CA: Quill Driver Books, 2007.

Duras, Marguerite. *The Lover*. New York: Pantheon Books, 1985.

Elbow, Peter. *Writing without Teachers*. New York: Oxford University Press, 1973.

Epel, Naomi. *Writers Dreaming: Twenty-Six Writers Talk about Their Dreams and the Creative Process*. New York: Carol Southern Books, 1993. Chaps. "Allan Gurganus," "Clive Barker," and "Richard Ford."

Ewart, Neil, ed. *The Writer and the Reader: A Book of Literary Quotations*. Poole, UK: Blandford Press, 1984.

Field, Joanna. *A Life of One's Own*. Los Angeles: Tarcher, 1981.

Fiffer, Sharon Sloan, and Steve Fiffer, eds. *Body: Writers Reflect on Parts of the Body*. New York: Harper Perennial, 2000.

Flynn, Nick. *Another Bullshit Night in Suck City: A Memoir*. New York: Norton, 2004.

Friedman, Bonnie. *Writing Past Dark: Envy, Fear, Distraction, and Other Dilemmas in the Writer's Life*. New York: HarperCollins, 1993.

Gardner, Jason, ed. *The Sacred Earth: Writers on Nature & Spirit*. Novato, CA: New World Library, 1998.

Gilchrist, Ellen. *Falling through Space: The Journals of Ellen Gilchrist*. Boston: Little, Brown, 1987.

Ginzburg, Natalia. "Worn-Out Shoes." In *The Little Virtues*, translated by Dick Davis. New York: Arcade, 1989.

Goldberg, Natalie. *Wild Mind: Living the Writer's Life*. New York: Bantam Books, 1990.

Goodman, Allegra. "Calming the Inner Critic and Getting to Work." In New York Times, *More Collected Essays*.

Hampl, Patricia. "The Need to Say It." In *The Writer on Her Work*, vol. 2, *New Essays in New Territory*, edited by Janet Sternburg. New York: Norton, 1991.

Harjo, Joy. *The Woman Who Fell from the Sky: Poems*. New York: Norton, 1996.

Harrison, Colin. "The Master Bedroom." In *Home: American Writers Remember Rooms of Their Own*, edited by Sharon Sloan Fiffer and Steve Fiffer. New York: Pantheon Books, 1995.

Hathaway, Katharine Butler. *The Little Locksmith: A Memoir*. New York: Feminist Press, 2000.

Heighton, Steven. "Given to Inspiration." In Bland, *Finding the Words*.

Heti, Sheila. *How Should a Person Be? A Novel from Life*. New York: Henry Holt, 2012.

Hirshfield, Jane. *Nine Gates: Entering the Mind of Poetry*. New York: Harper Perennial, 1998.

Homes, A. M. "Seeing the Unimaginable Freezes the Imagination." In *New York Times, More Collected Essays*.

Hornbacher, Marya. *Madness: A Bipolar Life*. Boston: Houghton Mifflin, 2008.

Isherwood, Christopher. *Diaries*. Vol. 2, *The Sixties: 1960–1969*. Edited by Katherine Bucknell. New York: HarperCollins, 2010.

Jung, C. G. "Man and Woman." In *C. G. Jung, Psychological*

Reflections: A New Anthology of His Writings, 1905–1961, edited by Jolande Jacobi and R. F. C. Hull. Princeton, NJ: Princeton University Press, 1973.

Jurgensen, Geneviève. *The Disappearance: A Memoir of Loss*. Translated by Adriana Hunter. New York: Norton, 1999.

Karr, Mary. *The Liars' Club: A Memoir*. New York: Penguin Books, 2005.

Keyes, Ralph. *The Courage to Write: How Writers Transcend Fear*. New York: Henry Holt, 1995.

King, Stephen. *On Writing: A Memoir of the Craft*. New York: Scribner, 2000.

Kingston, Maxine Hong. *To Be the Poet*. Cambridge, MA: Harvard University Press, 2002.

Kittredge, William. "Leaving the Ranch." In *The Next Rodeo: New and Selected Essays*. Saint Paul, MN: Graywolf Press, 2007.

Knize, Perri. *Grand Obsession: A Piano Odyssey*. New York: Scribner, 2008.

Kois, Dan. "Lynda Barry Will Make You Believe in Yourself." *New York Times*, October 27, 2011. www.nytimes .com/2011/10/30/magazine/cartoonist-lynda-barry -will-make-you-believe-in-yourself.html.

Kooser, Ted. *Lights on a Ground of Darkness: An Evocation of a Place and Time*. Lincoln: University of Nebraska Press, 2005.

Kusz, Natalie. "Scar Tissue." In Fiffer and Fiffer, *Body*.

Lahiri, Jhumpa. "My Life's Sentences." *New York Times*, March 17, 2012. http://opinionator.blogs.nytimes.com /2012/03/17/my-lifes-sentences/.

Lamott, Anne. *Bird by Bird: Some Instructions on Writing and Life*. New York: Pantheon Books, 1994.

Langella, Frank. *Dropped Names: Famous Men and Women as I Knew Them*. New York: Harper, 2012.

Lear, Frances. *The Second Seduction*. New York: Knopf, 1992.

Lebowitz, Fran. *Social Studies*. New York: Random House, 1981.

L'Engle, Madeleine. *Madeleine L'Engle Herself: Reflections on a Writing Life*. Compiled by Carole F. Chase. Colorado Springs: Shaw Books, 2001.

———. *Two-Part Invention: The Story of a Marriage*. New York: HarperCollins, 1989.

Lopate, Phillip, ed. *The Art of the Personal Essay: An Anthology from the Classical Era to the Present*. New York: Anchor Books, 1995.

Lyall, Sarah. "Caitlin Moran: 'Congratulations, You're a Feminist!'" *New York Times*, July 12, 2012. www.nytimes.com /2012/07/15/magazine/caitlin-moran-congratulations -youre-a-feminist.html.

Lynch, Thomas. *Bodies in Motion and at Rest: On Metaphor and Mortality*. New York: Norton, 2000.

Mairs, Nancy. *Voice Lessons: On Becoming a (Woman) Writer*. Boston: Beacon Press, 1997.

May, Rollo. *The Courage to Create*. New York: Norton, 1975.

Mendelsohn, Jane. "Amelia Earhart, Found and Lost." *New York Times*, June 9, 2012. www.nytimes.com/2012/06/10 /opinion/sunday/amelia-earhart-found-and-lost.html.

Mernit, Billy. *Writing the Romantic Comedy: From "Cute Meet" to "Joyous Defeat"; How to Write Screenplays That Sell*. New York: HarperResource, 2001.

Mitchell, Sean. "United Offstage, Separated On." *Los Angeles Times*, February 12, 2012. http://articles.latimes.com /2012/feb/12/entertainment/la-ca-harris-madigan -henley-20120212.

Moehringer, J. R. *The Tender Bar: A Memoir*. New York: Hyperion, 2005.

Monette, Paul. *Last Watch of the Night: Essays Too Personal and Otherwise*. New York: Harcourt, Brace, 1994.

Moody, Rick. "Demonology." In *Survival Stories: Memoirs of*

Crisis, edited by Kathryn Rhett. New York: Doubleday, 1997.

Moore, Dinty W. *Crafting the Personal Essay: A Guide for Writing and Publishing Creative Nonfiction*. Cincinnati: Writer's Digest Books, 2010.

Morrow, Susan Brind. *The Names of Things: A Passage in the Egyptian Desert*. New York: Riverhead Books, 1997.

Moschovakis, Anna. *You and Three Others Are Approaching a Lake*. Minneapolis: Coffee House Press, 2011.

Mosley, Walter. *This Year You Write Your Novel*. New York: Little, Brown, 2007.

Moyers, Bill. *The Language of Life: A Festival of Poets*. Edited by James Haba. New York: Doubleday, 1995. Chaps. "David Mura" and "Stanley Kunitz."

Murakami, Haruki. *What I Talk about When I Talk about Running: A Memoir*. Translated by Philip Gabriel. New York: Vintage International, 2009.

Murdock, Maureen. *Unreliable Truth: On Memoir and Memory*. New York: Seal Press, 2003.

Naipaul, V. S. "Congo River Journal." In *Our Private Lives: Journals, Notebooks, and Diaries*, edited by Daniel Halpern. New York: Vintage Books, 1990.

Nash, Jennie. *The Victoria's Secret Catalog Never Stops Coming: And Other Lessons I Learned from Breast Cancer*. New York: Scribner, 2003.

Neruda, Pablo. *The Book of Questions*. Translated by William O'Daly. 2nd ed. Port Townsend, WA: Copper Canyon Press, 2001.

New York Times, ed. *Writers on Writing*. Vol. 2, *More Collected Essays from the* New York Times. New York: Times Books, 2003.

Norris, Kathleen. *Amazing Grace: A Vocabulary of Faith*. New York: Riverhead Books, 1998.

———. *Dakota: A Spiritual Geography*. Boston: Mariner Books, 2001.

Nye, Naomi Shihab. "You Know Who You Are." In *Words under the Words: Selected Poems*. Portland, OR: Eighth Mountain Press, 1995.

Oates, Joyce Carol. *The Faith of a Writer: Life, Craft, Art*. New York: Ecco, 2004.

Obama, Barack. *Dreams from My Father: A Story of Race and Inheritance*. New York: Three Rivers Press, 2004.

O'Donohue, John. *To Bless the Space between Us: A Book of Blessings*. New York: Doubleday, 2008.

Oliver, Mary. *Blue Pastures*. New York: Harcourt, Brace, 1995.

Packer, ZZ. "Mad Hope and Mavericks." In Benedict, *Mentors, Muses & Monsters*.

Palumbo, Dennis. "Commitment to the Creative Life." *Hollywood on the Couch*, January 24, 2012. www.psychologytoday.com/blog/hollywood-the-couch/201201/commitment-the-creative-life.

Phillips, Adam. *Monogamy*. New York: Pantheon Books, 1997.

Piercy, Marge. "To Be of Use." In *Fooling with Words: A Celebration of Poets and Their Craft*, edited by Bill Moyers. New York: Morrow, 1999.

Pressfield, Steven. *The War of Art: Winning the Inner Creative Battle*. New York: Rugged Land, 2002.

Radziwill, Carole. *What Remains: A Memoir of Fate, Friendship & Love*. New York: Scribner, 2005.

Rainer, Tristine. *Your Life as Story: Discovering the "New Autobiography" and Writing Memoir as Literature*. New York: Tarcher/Putnam, 1998.

Rhodes, Richard. *How to Write: Advice and Reflections*. New York: Morrow, 1995.

Richards, Keith. *Life*. New York: Back Bay Books, 2011.

Richards, M. C. *Centering in Pottery, Poetry, and the Person*. 2nd ed. Middletown, CT: Wesleyan University Press, 1989.

Richards, Susan. *Chosen by a Horse: How a Broken Horse Fixed a Broken Heart*. Orlando, FL: Harcourt, 2007.

Roiphe, Anne. *Epilogue: A Memoir*. New York: Harper, 2008.

Bibliography

Roland, Gwen. *Atchafalaya Houseboat: My Years in the Louisiana Swamp*. Baton Rouge: Louisiana State University Press, 2006.

Salzman, Mark. *The Man in the Empty Boat*. New York: Open Road, 2012.

Sedaris, David. *When You Are Engulfed in Flames*. New York: Little, Brown, 2008.

See, Carolyn. *Making a Literary Life: Advice for Writers and Other Dreamers*. New York: Random House, 2002.

Shapiro, Dani. *Slow Motion: A Memoir of a Life Rescued by Tragedy*. New York: Harper Perennial, 2010.

Simpson, Marita, and Martha Wheelock, eds. *May Sarton: A Self-Portrait*. New York: Norton, 1986.

Skloot, Floyd. *The Wink of the Zenith: The Shaping of a Writer's Life*. Lincoln: University of Nebraska Press, 2008.

Smith, Patti. *Just Kids*. New York: Ecco, 2010.

Sonnenberg, Susanna. *Her Last Death: A Memoir*. New York: Scribner, 2008.

Sontag, Susan. *I, Etcetera*. New York: Farrar, Straus and Giroux, 1978.

Stafford, William. *Writing the Australian Crawl: Views on the Writer's Vocation*. Ann Arbor: University of Michigan Press, 1978.

Steinbeck, John. *Journal of a Novel: The East of Eden Letters*. New York: Penguin Books, 1990.

St. John, Linda. *Even Dogs Go Home to Die: A Memoir*. New York: HarperCollins, 2001.

Strayed, Cheryl. *Wild: From Lost to Found on the Pacific Crest Trail*. New York: Knopf, 2012.

Sussman, Ellen. "A Writer's Daily Habit: Four Steps to Higher Productivity." *Poets & Writers*, November/December 2011.

Szymborska, Wislawa. *Monologue of a Dog: New Poems*. Translated by Clare Cavanagh and Stanislaw Baranczak. Orlando, FL: Harcourt, 2006.

Tharp, Twyla. *The Creative Habit: Learn It and Use It for Life; A Practical Guide*. New York: Simon & Schuster, 2003.

Theroux, Phyllis. *The Journal Keeper: A Memoir*. New York: Atlantic Monthly Press, 2010.

Thomas, Abigail. *Safekeeping: Some True Stories from a Life*. New York: Anchor Books, 2001.

————. *Thinking about Memoir*. New York: Sterling, 2008.

Tolle, Eckhart. *Guardians of Being*. Novato, CA: New World Library, 2009.

Tuck, Lily. "The Seducer." In Benedict, *Mentors, Muses & Monsters*.

Ueland, Brenda. *If You Want to Write: A Book about Art, Independence and Spirit*. 2nd ed. Saint Paul, MN: Graywolf Press, 1987.

Ventura, Michael. "The Ex-Files." In *Men on Divorce: The Other Side of the Story*, edited by Penny Kaganoff and Susan Spano. New York: Harcourt, Brace, 1997.

Watson, Larry. *Montana 1948: A Novel*. Minneapolis: Milkweed, 1993.

"Where Do Poets Get Their Inspiration?" *O, the Oprah Magazine*, April 2011. www.oprah.com/spirit/Where -Poems-Come-From-Inspiration-for-Poetry.

White, Edmund. *Jack Holmes and His Friend: A Novel*. New York: Bloomsbury, 2012.

Wiggins, Marianne. *The Shadow Catcher: A Novel*. New York: Simon & Schuster, 2007.

Zinsser, William. *On Writing Well: An Informal Guide to Writing Nonfiction*. New York: Harper & Row, 1976.

INDEX OF ARTISTS QUOTED

Index of Artists Quoted

ABOUT THE AUTHOR

Barbara Abercrombie has published novels, children's picture books, such as the award-winning *Charlie Anderson*, and books of nonfiction. Her personal essays have appeared in national publications as well as in many anthologies. She received the Outstanding Instructor Award and the Distinguished Instructor Award at UCLA Extension, where she teaches creative writing in the Writers' Program. She also conducts private writing retreats and writes a weekly blog at www.WritingTime.typepad.com. She lives with her husband, Robert V. Adams, and their rescue dog, Nelson, in Santa Monica and Lake Arrowhead, California.

A portion of the royalties for this book will be donated to WriteGirl, a nonprofit organization that helps teenage girls write their way to more positive futures (www .WriteGirl.org).

NEW WORLD LIBRARY is dedicated to publishing books and other media that inspire and challenge us to improve the quality of our lives and the world.

We are a socially and environmentally aware company, and we strive to embody the ideals presented in our publications. We recognize that we have an ethical responsibility to our customers, our staff members, and our planet.

We serve our customers by creating the finest publications possible on personal growth, creativity, spirituality, wellness, and other areas of emerging importance. We serve New World Library employees with generous benefits, significant profit sharing, and constant encouragement to pursue their most expansive dreams.

As a member of the Green Press Initiative, we print an increasing number of books with soy-based ink on 100 percent postconsumer-waste recycled paper. Also, we power our offices with solar energy and contribute to nonprofit organizations working to make the world a better place for us all.

Our products are available
in bookstores everywhere.
For our catalog, please contact:

New World Library
14 Pamaron Way
Novato, California 94949

Phone: 415-884-2100 or 800-972-6657
Catalog requests: Ext. 50
Orders: Ext. 52
Fax: 415-884-2199
Email: escort@newworldlibrary.com

To subscribe to our electronic newsletter, visit:
www.newworldlibrary.com

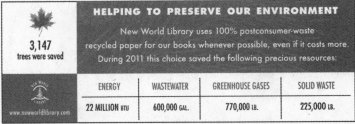

HELPING TO PRESERVE OUR ENVIRONMENT

3,147 trees were saved

New World Library uses 100% postconsumer-waste recycled paper for our books whenever possible, even if it costs more. During 2011 this choice saved the following precious resources:

ENERGY	WASTEWATER	GREENHOUSE GASES	SOLID WASTE
22 MILLION BTU	600,000 GAL.	770,000 LB.	225,000 LB.

www.newworldlibrary.com

Environmental impact estimates were made using the Environmental Defense Fund Paper Calculator @ www.papercalculator.org.